PROBLEMS AND PERSPECTIVES IN HISTORY
EDITOR: H. F. KEARNEY, M.A., PH.D.

The Dreyfus Affair

PROBLEMS AND PERSPECTIVES IN HISTORY
EDITOR: H. F. KEARNEY, M.A., PH.D.

Titles in this series will include:
BRITAIN AND GERMANY BETWEEN THE WARS
ORIGINS OF THE SCIENTIFIC REVOLUTION
THE RENAISSANCE
SOCIAL CHANGE AND REVOLUTION IN 17TH CENTURY ENGLAND
THE ENLIGHTENMENT
LOUIS XIV
THE AMERICAN CIVIL WAR
THE ROMANTIC MOVEMENT
ORIGINS OF THE INDUSTRIAL REVOLUTION
THE ITALIAN RISORGIMENTO
THE NEW DEAL 1933–1939
ORIGINS OF PARLIAMENT
THE MODERN EUROPEAN MIND
THE THIRTIES

The Dreyfus Affair

Catalyst for Tensions in French Society

H. R. Kedward, M.A., B.Phil.

ASSISTANT LECTURER IN HISTORY
UNIVERSITY OF SUSSEX

LONGMANS

LONGMANS, GREEN AND CO LTD
48 Grosvenor Street, London W1
*Associated companies, branches and representatives
throughout the world*

© H. R. Kedward 1965
First published 1965

*Printed in Great Britain by Richard Clay (The Chaucer Press), Ltd.,
Bungay, Suffolk*

Editor's Foreword

'Study problems in preference to periods' was the excellent advice given by Lord Acton in his inaugural lecture at Cambridge. To accept it is one thing, to put it into practice is another. In fact, in both schools and universities the teaching of history, in depth, is often hindered by certain difficulties of a technical nature, chiefly to do with the availability of sources. In this respect, history tends to be badly off in comparison with literature or the sciences. The historical equivalents of set texts, readings, or experiments, in which the student is encouraged to use his own mind, are the so-called 'special periods'. If these are to be fruitful, the student must be encouraged to deal in his own way with the problems raised by historical documents and the historiography of the issues in question and he must be made aware of the wider perspectives of history. Thus, if the enclosure movement of the sixteenth century is studied, the student might examine the historiographical explanations stretching from More's *Utopia* and Cobbett to Beresford's *Lost Villages of England*. At the same time he might also be dealing with selected documents raising important problems. Finally he might be encouraged to realize the problems of peasantries at other periods of time, including Russia and China in the nineteenth and twentieth centuries. In this particular instance, thanks to Tawney and Power, *Tudor Economic Documents*, the history teacher is comparatively well off. For other special periods the situation is much more difficult. If, however, the study of history is to encourage the development of the critical faculties as well as the memory, this approach offers the best hope. The object of this series is to go some way towards meeting these difficulties.

The general plan of each volume in the series will be similar, with a threefold approach from aspects of historiography, documents and editorial consideration of wider issues, though the structure and balance between the three aspects may vary.

A broad view is being taken of the limits of history. Political history will not be excluded, but a good deal of emphasis will be placed on economic, intellectual and social history. The idea has in fact grown out of the experience of a group of historians at the University of Sussex, where the student is encouraged to investigate the frontier areas between his own and related disciplines.

H. Kearney

Acknowledgements

I would like to thank my family, my fiancée, my tutors and friends at Oxford, Hugh Kearney and other colleagues at Sussex, and Mrs Pat Kirkpatrick, who typed the manuscript, for all their help and stimulus, and Longmans, Green & Co for their suggestions and assistance.

H. R. K.

We are grateful to the following for permission to reproduce copyright material:

George Allen & Unwin Ltd for material from *The Dreyfus Case* by F. C. Conybeare; The Bodley Head Ltd for material from *Jean Barois* by R. Martin du Gard; Calmann-Levy Editeurs for material from *L'île des Pingouins* by A. France; William Collins Sons & Co Ltd for material from *Notre Jeunesse* by Charles Péguy; Fasquelle Editeurs for material from *Histoire de l'affaire Dreyfus* by J. Reinach; Librairie Ernest Flammarion for material from *Confession d'un Vieux Diplomate* by Comte de Saint Aulaire; Le Figaro Littéraire for an extract from C. Péguy's letter to Millerand, 13 January 1898; Editions Gallimard for material from *Souvenirs sur l'Affaire* by L. Blum, © Editions Gallimard; Robert Hale Ltd for material from *France 1940–55* by Alexander Werth; the Executors of the Estate of the late Charles Maurras for material from *L'Enquête sur la Monarchie* by Charles Maurras; Librairie Plon for material from *Scènes et doctrines du Nationalisme* by Maurice Barrès and *Ce que mes yeux ont vu* by A. Meyer; Librairie Aristide Quillet for material from *L'Affaire Dreyfus: l'iniquité, la réparation* by L. Leblois; Editions Rieder for material from *Carnets* by Colonel Schwartzkoppen; Librairie Marcel Rivière et Cie for material from *La Révolution Dreyfusienne* by G. Sorel, and Editions Stock for material from *L'Iniquité* by G. Clemenceau, *Catéchisme Dreyfusard* by J. Lemazurier, *L'Affaire Dreyfus et la mentalité catholique en France* by Saint-Poli H (abbé Brugerette), *Le Monument Henry* by P. Quillard *Drumont et Dreyfus* by L'Archiviste.

While every effort has been made we have been unable to trace the owners of certain copyright material included in this book, and any information that would enable us to do so would be greatly appreciated.

Contents

Editor's Foreword — v

PART ONE: A Divided Nation — 1
    Sources — 18

PART TWO: The Affair as a Catalyst

I Nationalist Tensions — 27
    Sources — 34

II Racial Tensions — 50
    Sources — 57

III Religious Tensions — 71
    Sources — 77

IV Political Tensions — 90
    Sources — 95

PART THREE: The Affair in History — 111
    Sources — 120

Index — 137

Illustrations

The following cartoons come from the anti-Dreyfusard *Le Psst!* and the Dreyfusard *Le Sifflet*, both of which appeared weekly, *Le Psst!* beginning on 5 February and *Le Sifflet* on 17 February 1898.

1. 'Cedant arma togae'. Forain. *Le Psst!* 19 February 1898   21
The Zola trial (February 1898), seen as an assault on the army by Zola's counsel ('Arms must give way to the habits of peace,' Cicero). The caption: 'And we put up with this!'

2. 'Allons-y'. Ibels. *Le Sifflet.* 24 February 1898   33
The Zola trial, seen as an assault on the principles of justice by Colonel Henry ('Let's get on with it!'). 'And we put up with *this*!'

3. 'La Dernière Quille'. Caran D'Ache. *Le Psst!*
5 February 1898   53
Everything (industry, commerce, etc) has fallen to the Jews except the army ('The last skittle'). Zola is their weapon to destroy this last bastion of France.

4. 'Est-ce une Croix ou un Sabre?' Ibels. *Le Sifflet.*
10 March 1898   74
Anti-Dreyfusism seen as an alliance of church and army. The people led by the clergy bow down to worship, but, asks the rational man, 'is it a cross or a sword?'

5. 'Esterhazy Ier! Pourquoi pas?' Ibels. *Le Sifflet.*
17 February 1898   98
Esterhazy's acquittal on 11 January 1898 was popular. The first cartoon in *Le Sifflet* portrays the danger to the régime. Is Esterhazy the new Boulanger or Bonaparte? 'Why not?'

6. 'Cassation'. Forain. *Le Psst!* 9 April 1898   116
On 2 April 1898 the verdict given on Zola in February was quashed by the Court of Appeal (cour de Cassation). Punning on the word 'Cassation', Forain shows the national flag being broken by a judge from the Appeal Court who is noticeably a Jew.

Part One
A DIVIDED NATION

I

'It is doubtful whether Dreyfus would ever have been a Dreyfusard.' This paradox noted by several contemporaries and historians is a familiar one. When he returned in 1899 from his imprisonment on Devil's Island, Dreyfus was a disappointment to many of his ardent supporters: he appeared too involved in his own suffering, and his military personality seemed out of key with the aspects of Dreyfusism which had developed during his absence from France. And introduced to the society of the salons he was just dull. Marcel Proust gives to the Duchesse de Guermantes the remark 'What a pity we can't choose someone else for our innocent'.[1] As Maurice Barrès observed, Dreyfus was a symbol, not only for the Dreyfusards but also for their opponents. It is true that the personal suffering of Dreyfus brought protests and sympathy: his poignant letters to his wife were published in several collections, and the appeals of his family and intimate friends were widely publicised. Similarly, those who opposed his cause often became personal detractors, and infamous stories of his private life, mostly drawn from another Dreyfus, found a ready public.

But Dreyfus the man was eclipsed by Dreyfus the symbol. He may have been seen as culprit, victim, martyr or hero, and technically the question ranged round his guilt or innocence, but the Dreyfus Affair was of infinitely wider significance. The problem for the historian is not only 'Who *did* betray France in 1894?' but also 'What was really at issue in the Dreyfus Affair?' and it is this second problem which is the central one here. It has caused considerable controversy, mostly at the time of the Affair itself or immediately afterwards. Participants advanced rival explanations for the Affair from the moment it began to divide France. It was seen variously as a Jewish

[1] Quoted by G. D. Painter: *Marcel Proust*, 1959, Vol. I, p. 248.

or a Jesuit plot, as a crisis for democracy or a threat to national unity, as an explosion of republican ideals or the opportunity for a monarchist revival. These and other interpretations of the Affair will be examined in the text and quoted in the documents. Such a multitude of conflicting opinions needed to be organised into coherent sections. An attempt has been made to achieve this coherence by superimposing a view of the Affair as a catalyst for tensions in French society.

Abbé Brugerette, one of the most eloquent among the small band of Catholic Dreyfusards, wrote in 1904:

> The Affair was like a sore which broke out suddenly on a sick body, on an organism in which the blood, weakened and polluted by disease, was decomposing. What was serious was the deep organic sickness of which the sore was the visible and definite sign.[1]

The metaphor may be extravagant and its emotive nature makes it questionable as history. What it achieves is a vivid picture of the Affair as an outburst of expression, an outburst which dramatically exposed the tensions underlying France. These tensions and their expressions, which are also in most cases individual or group interpretations of the Affair, are the concern of the chapters forming Part Two. For example, one of the major tensions is that between Jews and antisemites, and when Edouard Drumont ascribes the Affair to the machinations of the Jews he is both expressing this tension and also putting forward an interpretation of the Affair. Polemic and analysis were combined.

The controversy about the Affair is much more one among participants than one among historians; but certain divisions of opinion continued after Dreyfus was pardoned, and in Part Three the conflicting accounts since 1899 of the significance and meaning of the Affair are discussed. In Part One a brief background to the Affair and an equally brief survey of its events are given, followed by an analysis of the methods by which opinions were expressed.

The sources have been separated from the text but are integral to it. The reason for their selection has been the wish to underline first the conflict of opinion and secondly its complexity. A great number come from journalistic articles or rhetorical speeches. It was felt that their colour and vitality as well as their idioms would be sadly impaired in translation, and that the essential Frenchness of the Affair would be

[1] Henri de Saint-Poli (Abbé J. Brugerette): *L'Affaire Dreyfus et la mentalité catholique en France*, 1904, p. 107.

lost. They have therefore been left in the original but with an explanation and summary to make them as accessible as possible.

Throughout the book there is an attempt to give wide perspectives to the problem and the tensions which are being studied. Naturally most of these perspectives are found in the history of modern France which precedes and follows the Affair. In particular, frequent allusion is made to the period of Vichy and the Resistance. This period, together with the Dreyfus Affair, form the two major crises in recent French history when the divisions within France can best be examined. But one should also look beyond France, and it is hoped that the few suggestions of possible parallels which conclude the last chapter will help the reader to place the Dreyfus Affair in its widest context.

II

Since 4 September 1870, the day on which defeat by Bismarck's army became certain, France had been a Republic. Unlike the later Weimar Republic of Germany which was also born out of military defeat, the legacy of national disaster was not fatal to the régime, but between 1870 and 1900 it went through a number of crises which threatened its existence.

First, in the 1870s the claim that a Republic was the best successor to the Second Empire was strongly contested. Monarchists were returned in a majority to the first National Assembly, and through the government of the Duc de Broglie and the Presidency of General MacMahon attempts were made to secure a Bourbon restoration. But the monarchists were divided, and in the end they lacked the prime requisite, a monarch. On the other hand, the republicans had a Republic and the *de facto* existence of the régime was gradually accepted by the electorate. In 1877 the Third Republic had its first truly republican government, highly conscious of its powers and determined to subjugate the forces that had nearly overthrown the young régime. The social groups behind the monarchists had been dominantly Catholic, and in consequence the republicans launched a series of anticlerical measures to curb Catholic influence in society. Mainly under the influence of Jules Ferry, the Republic was given a secular, anticlerical character which alienated a significant percentage of the country. The conflict was focused on education: a struggle for the minds of the younger generation. But although the government by their legislative power could decree the disintegration of Catholic education, it was unable to make France a united secular society. On the contrary, tensions were aggravated.

The Boulanger threat in 1889 was the second major crisis. The romantic General gained his popularity as Minister of War by defiance of Bismarck. It was apparent that the catastrophe of 1870 was not forgotten. Against the complexity of republican politics and ministerial instability the General stood out like Napoleon in 1799 and his nephew in 1851. He was a figurehead, a man whose appeal bypassed the politicians and went straight to the people: he appeared to promise glory for France and a future of simple authority, but the absence of genuine political ability was in the end a fatal weakness. His support against the government, which tried to exclude him from power, was inchoate: it included most of the dissidents in society, from radicals wanting a more democratic constitution to Catholics demanding a revocation of the educational laws. He was financed by aristocrats: he was mobbed by crowds. Boulangism was thus initially a movement of the discontented at a moment when the government's hold on public opinion was slender. But it developed into a more specific threat as the General became an expression of political conservatism, the hope of Bonapartists and the tool of certain monarchists and clericals. When his courage failed and he fled to Belgium it was these forces in France who remained frustrated and disgruntled. In particular, those like Déroulède who had looked to the General to provide a new nationalism based on military glory were left disorganised without a definite cause. If the threat of Boulanger the adventurer was slight, the threat of Boulangism was more serious, and continued into the two crises of the 1890s: the Panama scandal and the Dreyfus Affair.

In 1888 the Assembly had voted permission for the Panama Canal Company to buttress its falling fortunes by a large public loan. When the investors did not materialise in sufficient numbers the Company was forced into liquidation. In 1892 it was revealed that the Company's interests had been promoted by dishonest finance and a system of bribery. In the mass of accusations that followed, several republican deputies were said to have received bribes from wealthy Jewish financiers acting for the Company at the time of the vote in 1888.

Two Jews in particular were inculpated, Jacques de Reinach and Cornelius Herz, and among the incriminated deputies was Floquet, who had been prime minister during the Boulanger crisis. For the enemies of the Republic this scandal merely vindicated their belief that the régime was incurably corrupt and unable to promote an ordered and powerful France. The antisemite Edouard Drumont and the Boulangist deputy Paul Déroulède led the attack on the republican politicians, accusing, among others, the influential radical Clemenceau. Their polemic was closely parallel. Drumont attacked the Jews in French society as a cancerous growth: Déroulède diagnosed a lack of patriotism among the politicians. Together they demanded a new France purged of its internal weaknesses. Such a demand was not dissimilar to that of Catholics, who saw their traditional France undermined by secularism, nor of socialists, who charged the Republic with capitalist decadence. In 1892, whatever the complex relationship between them, these various forces of criticism severely endangered the life of the régime.

But between 1892 and the Dreyfus Affair the Republic began to recover. Economically there was greater prosperity and politically the challenge from Catholics diminished. Leo XIII, a Pope with a flair for reconciliation, had suggested that French Catholics should leave their monarchist illusions and rally to the Republic. For some this was unthinkable; the educational conflict had made compromise impossible. For a smaller number the idea of Catholic republicanism was realistic: only by entering republican politics, they argued, would the interests of Catholicism be defended. The Ralliement, however, remained a minority movement: it was poorly supported by both Catholic and non-Catholic opinion in the country. Suspicion and hostility were more widespread than Leo XIII had believed, but at least Catholics were no longer the inevitable enemies of the régime.

In foreign affairs the alliance with Russia in 1894, negotiated on a mutual apprehension of German power, was a more emphatic indication of strength. France had re-entered the international scene with confidence.

By the mid 1890s the Third Republic had survived longer than any régime since the Revolution. Despite the expectations and hopes of a wide variety of critics, it had emerged intact from a succession of internal crises. But the stability was superficial: the tensions in society, exacerbated by the successive crises, were unresolved.

III

The arrest and conviction of Dreyfus in the autumn and winter of 1894 did not at once divide the country. Accused of delivering military secrets to the Germans through Colonel Schwartzkoppen, the German Military Attaché in Paris, Dreyfus protested his innocence to an unbelieving court-martial held in camera, and to a public which viewed his military degradation with little sympathy. Against the background of the Franco-Russian alliance, which had estranged Germany and France, rumours of espionage had been persistent but only minor spies had been arrested. The trial of Captain Alfred Dreyfus, an artillery officer and the first Jew to enter the General Staff, was therefore something of a showpiece, exonerating the War Office from accusations of carelessness and incompetence. It was quickly accepted by press and public alike that Dreyfus had communicated secrets of considerable importance. In fact, the 'bordereau', on the strength of which Dreyfus had been arrested, made reference to nothing of vital military significance. It was a sheet of paper listing a collection of documents and sent either with them or in advance. Its destination had been the German Military Attaché, and how it reached the espionage department of the War Office is still in dispute. Written by hand and obviously drafted by an officer, it was examined in context with other intercepted or stolen messages and ascribed to Dreyfus, whose handwriting was not dissimilar. It appeared that a major traitor from within the very walls of the army establishment had been unearthed and brought to justice. His sentence of exile and imprisonment on Devil's Island seemed to many a lenient one. Among the later supporters of Dreyfus, Jean Jaurès the socialist leader accused the bourgeois class of favouring its own criminals: had Dreyfus been a member of the proletariat, such mercy would not have been shown. Clemenceau also believed firmly in the guilt of Dreyfus: a unanimous verdict from the court-martial was incontrovertible. As for Edouard Drumont, anti-Dreyfusard from first to last, the traitor could be no one but a Jew. Two years before, this one-time anticlerical, turned Catholic and anti-semite, had launched a series of attacks on Jewish officers in the columns of his newspaper *La Libre Parole*, and once he had been informed of the arrest of Dreyfus his paper was devoted to demanding the Jewish captain's conviction. Drumont saw no need to question the evidence, and his certainty increased when the family of the convicted man acted as he had predicted. They set in motion a campaign for revision which in the first three years drew in other Jews, notably the Zionist Bernard Lazare and Joseph Reinach, nephew of the crooked financier Baron Jacques de Reinach, notorious for his part in the Panama scandal. For Drumont and the antisemites the apparent solidarity of the Jews was once more a threat to the country. It was less easy for them to dismiss the revisionism of Scheurer-Kestner as a symptom of a Jewish plot, but although he was a respected senator of impeccable past he was by religion a Protestant. Arthur Ranc, another early Dreyfusard, had a reputation for extreme left-wing agitation since the days of the commune, and Clemenceau, whom he brought to the revisionist cause, had also been tainted by the Panama racketeering of 1892. Further, the first major intellectual adherent to revisionism was the prominent academic Gabriel Monod, and he, like his friend Scheurer-Kestner, was of Protestant belief. For those who revered the army as the pillar of an ordered and honest society, for those whose Catholic interests had suffered heavily at the hands of an anticlerical Republic in the past twenty years, for those with a tendency to antisemitism, the coincidence of certain Jews, Freethinkers and Protestants combining in a joint enterprise was suspect. To this extent the equivalence of Jew, Protestant and anticlerical with Dreyfusard, and of Nationalist, Catholic and antisemite with anti-Dreyfusard, was grounded in fact. The prominent protagonists of either side fitted these labels, and for the sake of their polemic they were reluctant to admit that there were, and could be, anti-Dreyfusard Jews and Catholic Dreyfusards, to mention only two of the possible combinations which have come to seem paradoxical.

The strength of the revisionists, which at times appeared minimal, depended on the growth of revisionism in the two institutions which between 1894 and 1898 upheld the *chose jugée*: the army and parliament. Mercier, the minister of war in 1894, and Boisdeffre, the Chief of General Staff, had every reason to avert a second trial, since they had secured the condemnation of Dreyfus on slender evidence and by introducing a secret dossier of papers to the judges of the court-martial without the knowledge of Dreyfus and his lawyers. It was therefore highly embarrassing to them that the new head of the espionage department, Colonel Picquart, should discover that the writing of the 'bordereau' was not that of Dreyfus but of Count

Esterhazy, an officer continually in debt and of indifferent loyalty to army and women alike. Picquart was quickly and strategically moved to Tunisia, and in his absence Colonel Henry, one of his subordinates and no personal friend, proceeded to arrange the file on Dreyfus by means of forgery and alteration, to demonstrate clearly the guilt of Dreyfus and the error of Picquart. Aware of these manoeuvres, Picquart entrusted his discoveries in June 1897 to a Parisian lawyer Maître Leblois, through whom they reached Scheurer-Kestner. Independent of this disclosure Lazare and the revisionists also reached the figure of Esterhazy. Bernard Lazare had sold posters reproducing the 'bordereau' and letters of Dreyfus side by side. One of Esterhazy's creditors recognised the handwriting and informed Mathieu Dreyfus, the brother of the convicted man, who had given up his career to pursue the revisionist cause. Thus by the autumn of 1897 revisionism outside and inside the army was linked. Its strength had doubled.

At the end of the year the scene was set for a double drama of detection and ideological conflict. Disagreement about the judgment of 1894 was not merely over the facts and procedure of the case but increasingly over its emotional and ideological implications. It was this second aspect which came to predominate in 1898. The year opened with the court-martial of Esterhazy, who had welcomed it in order to clear his name. He was rapidly acquitted: he could not be guilty of the same crime for which Dreyfus had been convicted. The War Office steadily refused to open a full-scale enquiry into the case. The Assembly was still behind the army. Detection was blocked.

Not so the ideological conflict. On 13 January *L'Aurore* printed Zola's open letter to the President of the Republic, Felix Faure. Under the arresting title of *J'accuse*, selected from the text by Clemenceau, the novelist who had brought a pungent and critical realism to literature which to many was both sacrilegious and pornographic, threw his reputation firmly on the side of revision. It was not his first Dreyfusard proclamation, but its blatant defiance and the extent of its accusations against the army made it sensational. Those in public and private who had remained aloof from the Affair were now intensely involved. Zola was anticlerical, antimilitarist, an egoist of the Hugo mould. The vehemence of his literature and personality created open divisions where before they had been dormant. If the Affair is seen as a catalyst, Zola's *J'accuse* is the prime catalysing force. The Dreyfusards now had more than a legal cause: the intrusion of Zola had pushed them into an ideological offensive.

Politicians were strongly affected in one way or the other by *J'accuse*, but, with the general election approaching, the sympathies that existed among them for Dreyfus and Zola were underplayed: they had little popular appeal. As it was, several Dreyfusards, including Jean Jaurès, were defeated at the polls. Zola had not established revisionism in the Assembly. This was achieved by the second *coup de théâtre* of 1898: the suicide of Colonel Henry on 31 August after his forgeries had been discovered within the War Office. The impact of this unexpected turn of events followed the double character of the drama. Detection was accelerated. Esterhazy fled to Belgium, Picquart was partially vindicated and the process of revision was accepted by the Assembly. Ideologically the anti-Dreyfusards, like the Dreyfusards after *J'accuse*, moved onto the offensive. Henry was justified as a patriot sacrificing his honour and life in the interests of army and nation.[1] Nationalism had received the impetus of martyrdom. In December the Ligue de la Patrie Française was founded to embody the new nationalist confidence. It stood opposed to the Ligue des Droits de l'Homme, created during the Zola trial in February 1898 as the intellectual expression of the Dreyfusard campaign.

Throughout 1899 the process of revision moved towards the return of Dreyfus, weak and ill after more than four years confinement, and his retrial by a court-martial sitting at Rennes. The verdict of 'guilty with extenuating circumstances' given by five judges out of seven was the last desperate self-justification of the army leaders. The trial had been a pageant of military values, and the immediate pardon given to Dreyfus by the government could not extinguish the anger and scorn of the Dreyfusards. Their triumph was to be not a legal but a political one. In the following six years their strength in the Assembly was harnessed to retribution. The social forces of the anti-Dreyfusards, in the army, the church, education and the press, were attacked by crippling legislation. It is this all-important sequel to the Affair which has been called the Dreyfusian Revolution. It concluded the detection when the Rennes verdict was quashed in 1906 by the Court of Appeal: it was yet another stage in the ideological conflict. The tensions played out in the Dreyfus Affair were in part mitigated, in part exacerbated in this period. Most of them continued to produce divisions in a France where the guilt or innocence of Dreyfus had not been the fundamental issue.

[1] See Sources, p. 41, no. 2, Maurras.

IV

There has been a tendency among many historians to see the Affair as a struggle of light against darkness, justice against injustice, progress against reaction. Such an interpretation is seductive. French history seems to be full of such dualisms. One could be for or against the Revolution, for or against Napoleon, for or against Dreyfus, for or against Marshal Pétain, and French opinion has been frequently polarised in this way. But the pattern of for and against has been deceptively converted into the more questionable dualism of right and wrong. Thus it is sometimes said that the Dreyfus Affair caused a division in France not only between those who were for Dreyfus and those who were against him, but also between those who saw clearly enough to be right and those who were prejudiced and wrong. Part of the appeal of the Dreyfus Affair lies in this apparent clarity. It invites a partisan approach. This would seem justified, since the verdict of 1906 vindicated Dreyfus, and subsequent revelations have proved that he was indeed innocent. But once it is accepted that the issue during the Affair was far wider than the guilt or innocence of Dreyfus, judgments about who was right and who was wrong become shallow. It is quickly apparent that such simplifications belie the complexity of the period.

One could, of course, compare Scheurer-Kestner's rational dedication to justice with the insidious fantasies of Edouard Drumont, and label them right and wrong or light and darkness. But other comparisons could be made less flattering to the Dreyfusard cause. For example, the anticlericalism of a Dreyfusard pamphleteer Jean Ajalbert looks dark and intolerant when compared with the caution of the moderate Catholic paper *L'Univers et le Monde*, which accepted the verdict on Dreyfus.[1] To prolong such examples would be only to underline the absurdity of unequal comparisons, but it is on such inequalities that many judgments have been based.

These judgments allotting praise and blame are even harder to justify when the methods used by Dreyfusards and anti-Dreyfusards are set together. Both sides used extremist polemic in the press, both had their pamphleteers and cartoonists, both appealed to the opinion

[1] See Sources, p. 86, no. 5; p. 78, no. 3.

of intellectuals, both permeated the salons, both organised leagues and activist groups.

The first of these methods, the intensive campaign through the press, is the hallmark of the Affair. From the moment when Mercier and the General Staff accelerated the prosecution of Dreyfus in apparent answer to the demands of the press, the subservience of politicians, lawyers and army leaders to the power of journalism was continuous. Only when Waldeck-Rousseau formed his ministry of republican solidarity and pardoned Dreyfus was control of events finally wrested from the editors and columnists. It had been the glorious age of French journalism. In the novel *Jean Barois* by Roger Martin du Gard, a fictitious account of the Affair which reads like fact, the young hero, an anticlerical doctor and disciple of the Dreyfusard cause, turned to journalism rather than politics.[1] The main protagonists of the Affair were almost all connected with a newspaper. Among the anti-Dreyfusard editors were Edouard Drumont of *La Libre Parole*, Père Bailly of *La Croix*, Judet of *Le Petit Journal*, Guillaume Sabatier of *L'Eclair*, Henri Rochefort of *L'Intransigeant* and Arthur Meyer of *Le Gaulois*, while Dreyfusard editors included Clemenceau and Ernest Vaughan of *L'Aurore*, Yves Guyot of *Le Siècle* and Jean Jaurès of *La Petite République*. Of the anti-Dreyfusard columnists Charles Maurras wrote for *La Gazette de France*, Maurice Barrès for *Le Journal*, and for the Dreyfusards Emile Zola and Bernard Lazare both wrote for *L'Aurore*.

The circulation of these newspapers told heavily for the anti-Dreyfusards. Although, with the publication of *J'accuse*, *L'Aurore* rose to a circulation of 200,000, this figure was dwarfed by the consistent 500,000 of *La Libre Parole* and the 1,500,000 of *Le Petit Journal*. No Dreyfusard paper could match the extensive network of *La Croix*, which penetrated by means of a hundred smaller publications into most areas of provincial France. Its main rival outside Paris was the Radical *La Dépêche de Toulouse*, but until 1899 its anticlericalism was joined to a belief in Dreyfus's guilt.

It would be easy to select extracts from the newspapers to accentuate a particular editor's skill in devising pungent headlines and thereby give the impression that the newspaper war was conducted in the admass style of mid-twentieth-century journalism. Although forerunners of this style can be found, it was an age of long articles, closely argued and closely printed. Zola's sensational *J'accuse* in *L'Aurore* ran to three thousand words, and the famous nationalist apology for Colonel

[1] See Sources, p. 20, no. 2.

Henry's forgeries by Charles Maurras in *La Gazette de France* was in two long parts with modest titling. Editorials were more concise and were normally signed, thus bringing into prominence not only the policy but also the personality of the editor. Few papers combined photographs and cartoons with their articles and news; it was more usual to run either an illustrated supplement or a weekly series of caricatures. In one of the more interesting products of the Affair, *L'Affaire et l'Image*, by J. Grand-Carteret, the author laments the decline of caricature to fanaticism and party politics. The great tradition of Daumier, Traviès, Monnier and Grandville was that of satirising the complacency and evils of society. This, he argued, had been lost with the exception of the drawings of F. Vallotton, one of which he reproduced with unmixed praise. It presented two farm workers, hoes in hand, against a background of darkening sky from which the distant rumble of the Affair can be imagined. And the caption read: '*Tout ça, c'est point de la justice, père Bridu, c'est de la politique.*' Such detached comment was rare, and even this cartoon appeared in the Dreyfusard publication *Le Sifflet*. The caricaturists' interest in the Affair had grown commensurate with the development of Scheurer-Kestner's campaign, but it was the suggestion of a Jewish plot, on the one hand, and of a Jesuit plot, on the other, which gave them their stereotypes. Jews with vast noses and priests exploiting the confessional proliferated. The meanings were explicit, the appeal basic. Only in a few publications of a higher artistic calibre, such as *Le Sifflet* and the anti-Dreyfusard *Le Psst!*, was the rôle of the reader a positive one. Directed at a more informed section of the public, they used suggestion, indirectness and frequent representation of the main characters of the Affair.

Journalists and cartoonists were buttressed in their campaigns by publicists of equally varying quality and potency. Since newspapers held articles of considerable length, other publications tended to fall into one of three categories. First, sensational revelations of pamphlet size, of which Esterhazy's *La vérité sur l'Affaire Dreyfus* is typical. It stopped just short of the Affair, with 'To be continued' predicting a sequel which never appeared. Second, statements or opinions from various leagues or parties, of which Brunetière's *La Nation et l'Armée*, published by the Ligue de la Patrie Française, is an example.[1] Third, anthologies of letters, sociological analyses and essays of interpretation which were in book form but with an immediately functional purpose.

[1] See Sources, p. 46, no. 2, Brunetière.

In this third category the publishing firm of P. V. Stock produced a stream of Dreyfusard literature. Stock's own memoirs reveal how central he was as a publisher to the unravelling of the Affair. He had overheard Forzinetti, the officer in charge of Dreyfus, testify to the innocence of his prisoner, and, convinced of this, gave every encouragement to Bernard Lazare by publishing his *L'Affaire Dreyfus. Une erreur judiciaire* in 1897. His position stated, he came to receive secret visits from often unknown characters revealing aspects of the Affair. One Edouard Autant brought him letters of Esterhazy, and a Pierre Fritel introduced him to one of Dreyfus's judges, Captain Freystätter, who told the publisher of the secret dossier. In such ways the underworld of the Affair came to the public. Compared with Stock's account, the memoirs of Henri Brisson, an important politician, are relatively uninformed.

The supremacy of the written word during the Dreyfus Affair was accompanied by an intellectual involvement which forced men of ideas, scholarship and creativity into divisions often rigid and permanent. Starting as a controversy over the guilt or innocence of Dreyfus and moving into a debate on the character and future of France, the Affair appealed, firstly, to the intellectual's sense of objectivity, and secondly, to his subjective ideas and prejudice. For those who have classified these intellectual participants into Dreyfusard and anti-Dreyfusard two lists of names have been particularly important.[1] The first was the list of those who supported the Dreyfusard manifesto in *L'Aurore* on 14 January 1898, the day after *J'accuse*. The title 'Manifesto of the Intellectuals' was yet another of Clemenceau's inspirations, but it was not such an unqualified success as his achievement of the previous day. The term intellectual was an easy one to ridicule: it provoked some of the more brilliant and caustic passages in Barrès. Moreover, in any numerical sense the manifesto was not exclusive, and it was not difficult for the anti-Dreyfusards to challenge its monopolistic claims. This was done decisively when the Ligue de la Patrie Française was formed in defence of army and nation in December 1898. In number the list of members made the Dreyfusard intellectuals of the manifesto appear a small minority faction, but during 1899 it was apparent that numbers were not everything. The Dreyfusard intellectuals were more united in policy than their opponents, and their aims had been more specific. All other comparisons between the two are liable to over-simplification, though the recognised view that

[1] See pp. 31–2.

the manifesto was the product mainly of students and university teachers from the Paris Left Bank, while the anti-Dreyfusards found their staunchest support from the immortals of the Académie Française can be cautiously repeated. The partisan attitudes of two major scholarly periodicals give support to this division. The *Revue des Deux Mondes*, the foremost intellectual organ of the Academicians, was closed to Dreyfusard sympathisers. In return the latter had exclusive use of the *Revue Blanche*.

One of the more interesting jousts in the intellectual tournament was that between Ferdinand Brunetière and Emile Duclaux. Both were eminent men of wide influence; Brunetière a man of letters and critic and a member of the Académie Française, Duclaux a scientist in the wake of Pasteur and a member of the Académie des Sciences. Asked by Scheurer-Kestner for his opinion as a savant on the conduct of the case, Duclaux had replied:

> I think quite simply that if in the scientific problems we have to resolve we conducted our research as it seems to have been conducted in this Affair, we would have arrived at the truth only by sheer chance.[1]

This scepticism of the case against Dreyfus grew into an article '*Propos d'un Solitaire*' (1898), where he developed the reasons for his statement, though hesitating to accuse the army of injustice. A little later Brunetière wrote '*Après le procès*'—a reply to 'a few intellectuals' where he was dauntless enough to charge science with some responsibility for the growth of antisemitism, on the argument that racialism increased when ethnography began to conceptualise it. Duclaux's answer, '*Avant le procès*', accused Brunetière of selectivity in his choice of evidence and inconsistency in his own ideas: a man with a name for liberal criticism, he stated, should really be a Dreyfusard. The conflict was moderate but firm, and the depth of conviction was evident.

In the Paris salons, on the other hand, divisions of opinion followed the flamboyant character of high society and frequently produced elaborate shows of temper and broken social relationships. In one evening at the fashionable salon of Mme Strauss Jules Lemaître, the later president of the Ligue de la Patrie Française, and Forain the cartoonist broke with Reinach and Proust after protesting against intemperate attacks on the army by other guests. In consequence, Lemaître became a regular diner at the rival salon of the Comtesse de

[1] E. Duclaux: *Propos d'un solitaire* 1898. Avant-propos, p. 4.

Loynes which attracted a large number of anti-Dreyfusards, including Arthur Meyer and Maurice Barrès. At this salon the announcement of Zola's *J'accuse* caused indignant consternation. 'This declaration of war,' wrote Meyer, 'was decisive. It compelled everyone to take sides in the struggle.'[1] A third salon and as Dreyfusard as that of Mme Strauss was the one belonging to Mme de Caillavet, with Anatole France and Marcel Prévost as the leading lights, and later able to boast the attendance of Emile Combes, whose legislation against Catholic interests between 1902 and 1905 sealed the triumph of the Dreyfusard anticlericals.

The last method of expression common to Dreyfusards and anti-Dreyfusards alike was the intensive organisation of leagues and activist groups to conduct public meetings, to publish polemical articles and if necessary to take the controversy into the streets. Two Leagues founded before the Affair provided recent precedents: the Ligue Antisémite dating from 1889 founded by Edouard Drumont and a violent fallen aristocrat the Marquis de Morès, and the Ligue des Patriotes led by Paul Déroulède, whose nationalist call for revenge against Germany had seemed to be answered by the advent of Boulanger. The timorous failure of this General led to the dissolution of the patriots, while Drumont's youths were first encouraged by the Panama scandal but grew less active with the decline of overt antisemitism in the two years before the arrest of Dreyfus. The Affair brought new life and purpose to both formations, and much of the anti-Dreyfusard violence came from one or other of these two leagues. But the group mentality was a phenomenon not only of the thugs of Morès and the nationalist ranks of Déroulède. Young Dreyfusards were organised on similar lines by students of the Left Bank, more particularly those under the influence of the socialist librarian Lucien Herr and the young idealist Charles Péguy. For example, they manned strategic points in the Paris streets at the funeral of President Faure on 23 February 1899, prepared to meet the followers of Déroulède should they stage a nationalist revolt. Déroulède tried and failed:[2] his attempt has been remembered. Péguy and his bands had no need to resort to violence, but their readiness to do so has been frequently forgotten.

Overshadowing these activist formations, the two great Leagues of the Affair, the Ligue des Droits de l'Homme and the Ligue de la Patrie Française, expressed the width and intensity of the controversy. Their

[1] A. Meyer: *Ce que je peux dire*, 1912, p. 248.
[2] See Part Two, chapter 4, Political Tensions.

conflicting ideals will be examined in Part Two, chapter 1, Nationalist Tensions, but it is necessary to stress in this section the similarity of their intentions to be an extraparliamentary pressure group, highly articulate and concerned not merely to express a view on the judgment of 1894 but also to advertise their particular views on the condition and future of France. The press on the whole fell into line behind the Leagues and promoted their propaganda. The individualist *Dépêche de Toulouse* makes an exception. On 9 January 1899 it stated:

> Leagues! What a mass of Leagues! And why? Just because an officer of the General Staff has been condemned more or less justly, more or less legally, are the triumphs of the French Revolution and the Rights of Man endangered? Why? Just because a number of publicists, professors and certain fanatics have believed they ought to work for the rehabilitation of a convicted man, is such an enterprise sufficient to imperil the Fatherland?

But the numbers of supporters continued to grow. The conflict encouraged the simplifications and depth of involvement necessary for group formations. To be a 'Ligueur' was to be committed, and the Dreyfus Affair was not a period of scepticism.

The continuity of these methods of expression, journalistic commitment, intellectual involvement and group activism in twentieth-century France is strong. Movements of Resistance against Vichy and the occupying Germans tended to begin with the publication of a newspaper. In conditions when production of a paper was an undertaking of extreme danger, the rôle of the journalist was yet as vital as during the Affair. The clandestine press, like the Dreyfusard press, was concerned, in varying degrees, with the truth of the situation and a particular vision of France. Most Resisters felt a deep need for both, and the tortuous efforts to distribute just one issue of a newspaper have been minutely described by several memoirists.[1] For Vichy there was less spontaneous journalism, though the deaf and embittered Charles Maurras continued his nationalist invective in the columns of *Action Française*—a journalism whose vitriolic hatred had lost much of the finesse of his anti-Dreyfusard campaign.

With Maurras there are others, like Léon Blum, who bridge the two great periods of division, and the tradition of intellectual involvement is itself a connecting factor. The names of Sartre, Camus, Malraux, Eluard, Aragon, Barbusse, Rolland, Bainville, to mention only a few, form part of the political as well as the intellectual history of twentieth-

[1] E.g. Emmanuel d'Astier: *Sept fois sept jours*, 1961 edition.

century France. In any country intellectuals tend to become involved in proportion to the ideological content of the nation's politics. In France the writings of the Encyclopaedists in the eighteenth century, the Revolution and the church–state conflicts have given to internal politics a lasting ideological character, which has been strengthened by the growth of socialism and communism, both ideological creeds. Even where the intellectuals have nothing in which to believe, their high status as men either employed by the state in universities or venerated publicly in the exalted Academies has tended to draw them into the political forum. With each crisis such as the Dreyfus Affair this involvement has crystallised. Intellectuals by their interest in ideas, diagnosis and expression find themselves almost by necessity on the political terrain.

Ideology breeds group formations, and a by-product of the ideological nature of French politics has been the proliferation of parties and leagues. Throughout the twentieth century the methods of group organisation and expression seen before but especially during the Dreyfus Affair continued. The Action Française stemming from the paper of that name became a permanent feature of French right-wing politics, flanked by other groups of a more exclusive and often mysterious character such as the Cagoulards of the 1930s—the Hooded Men. On the left the Resistance movements themselves were a climax of the league tradition. Such groups in recent French history are a comment on the limitations of the political parties. Where the parties could subsume and express a particular ideology the need for an extra-parliamentary group was removed. This was seen when the anti-fascist ideals of the 1930s were expressed by the parties of the Popular Front. But during the Affair and the Vichy period the parties either could not or would not assimilate all the ideals and beliefs of the time. Group formations were the direct result.

It is possible to conclude that the methods of political and ideological expression during the Affair show a certain uniformity. The passionate dialectic of the period lies not in a clash of methods but in the conflict of ideas. To this conflict the following chapters are directed.

SOURCES
Zola's 'J'accuse'

1. The Letter Itself

The accusations with which Zola ended his letter to President Faure were calculated to achieve the maximum sensation. By supplying the names of those he accused he felt confident of provoking a full enquiry into the whole case. In fact, he was prosecuted for only one of his charges, that against Esterhazy's court-martial, which he accused of acting under orders to cover the illegality of the judgment against Dreyfus. In this way Zola's prosecutors took the sting out of J'accuse and it was this clever limitation of the whole debate which aroused the indignation of Jaurès.[1] The conclusion of the letter reproduced here begins with Zola's clarion call, 'Truth is on the march, and nothing will stop it.' Then comes the summary of his accusations, which are not covered by this particular book, since it has not set out to examine the actual case in detail. However, the following points may give some context to the charges. Du Paty de Clam, the first and most heavily accused, was the officer who conducted the original investigation by which Dreyfus was arrested, and who carried out the cross-examination of Dreyfus. General Mercier was the minister of war at the time of the arrest and prosecution, and General Billot held the office between 1896 and 1898. General Boisdeffre, Chief of General Staff, and Gonse, his assistant, were officially responsible for supervising the investigation of the crime. General de Pellieux and Major Ravary led the enquiry into Esterhazy in December 1897, which was an important factor in his acquittal, while the three handwriting experts were those who testified in Esterhazy's favour when the authorship of the 'bordereau' was debated. The War Office is then accused of stimulating the press against Dreyfus, and the courts-martial of illegality. He concludes by willingly exposing himself to prosecution and denying that he has any personal rancour: his only passion is for truth.

J'ACCUSE

...Je le répète avec une certitude plus véhémente: la vérité est en marche, et rien ne l'arrêtera. C'est d'aujourd'hui seulement que l'affaire commence, puisqu'aujourd'hui seulement les positions sont nettes: d'une part, les coupables qui ne veulent pas que la justice se

[1] See Sources, p. 97, no. 2.

fasse; de l'autre, les justiciers qui donneront leur vie pour qu'elle soit faite...

Mais cette lettre est longue, Monsieur le Président, et il est temps de conclure:

J'accuse le lieutenant-colonel du Paty de Clam d'avoir été l'ouvrier diabolique de l'erreur judiciaire, en inconscient, je veux le croire, et d'avoir ensuite défendu son œuvre néfaste, depuis trois ans, par les machinations les plus saugrenues et les plus coupables.

J'accuse le général Mercier de s'être rendu complice, tout au moins par faiblesse d'esprit, d'une des plus grandes iniquités du siècle.

J'accuse le général Billot d'avoir eu entre les mains les preuves certaines de l'innocence de Dreyfus et de les avoir étouffées, de s'être rendu coupable de crime de lèse-humanité et de lèse-justice, dans un but politique et pour sauver l'Etat-Major compromis.

J'accuse le général de Boisdeffre et le général Gonse de s'être rendus complices du même crime, l'un sans doute par passion cléricale, l'autre peut-être par cet esprit de corps qui fait des bureaux de la Guerre l'arche sainte, inattaquable.

J'accuse le général de Pellieux et le commandant Ravary d'avoir fait une enquête scélérate, j'entends par là une enquête de la plus monstrueuse partialité, dont nous avons, dans le rapport du second, un impérissable monument de naïve audace.

J'accuse les trois experts en écritures, les sieurs Belhomme, Varinard et Couard, d'avoir fait des rapports mensongers et frauduleux, à moins qu'un examen médical ne les déclare atteints d'une maladie de la vue et du jugement.

J'accuse les bureaux de la Guerre d'avoir mené dans la presse, particulièrement dans *l'Eclair* et dans *l'Echo de Paris* une campagne abominable, pour égarer l'opinion et couvrir leur faute.

J'accuse, enfin, le premier Conseil de guerre d'avoir violé le droit, en condamnant un accusé sur une pièce restée secrète, et j'accuse le second Conseil de guerre d'avoir couvert cette illégalité par ordre, en commettant à son tour le crime juridique d'acquitter sciemment un coupable.

En portant ces accusations, je n'ignore pas que je me mets sous le coup des articles 30 et 31 de la loi sur la presse du 29 juillet 1881, qui punit les délits de diffamation. Et c'est volontairement que je m'expose.

Quant aux gens que j'accuse, je ne les connais pas, je ne les ai jamais vus, je n'ai contre eux ni rancune ni haine. Ils ne sont pour moi que des entités, des esprits de malfaisance sociale. Et l'acte que j'accomplis ici n'est qu'un moyen révolutionnaire pour hâter l'explosion de la vérité et de la justice.

Je n'ai qu'une passion, celle de la lumière, au nom de l'humanité qui a tant souffert et qui a droit au bonheur. Ma protestation enflammée n'est que le cri de mon âme. Qu'on ose donc me traduire en Cour d'assises, et que l'enquête ait lieu au grand jour!

J'attends.

Veuillez agréer, Monsieur le Président, l'assurance de mon profond respect.

EMILE ZOLA: *L'Aurore*, 13 January 1898.

2. Its Impact: A novelist's Account

The novel Jean Barois *by Roger Martin du Gard (1913) takes its theme directly from the Affair, or more widely from the conflict between traditional Catholicism and assertive scientific rationalism. It is written with a maximum of dialogue and printed like a play—in itself an apt reflection on the outburst of opinions and verbal expressions during the Affair. But in this extract description predominates, vivid and emotive. The publication of* J'accuse *is put into fiction. Luce is the Zola figure and* Le Semeur, *edited by Jean Barois, bears some resemblance at this point to L'Aurore, edited by Clemenceau. The other names mentioned are not important for this extract. Luce tells Barois that his one interest is to secure an open debate on the Affair and hesitantly asks if* Le Semeur *would carry his article. The impetuous pride of Barois leads Luce to warn him of the possible consequences, but their mutual dedication brings intimate agreement. In eight days the special edition of* Le Semeur *is ready: distribution begins and the cries of the vendors echo through the streets and along the quays. Pedestrians stop and reach for copies, which are dispersed as if by a storm. The vendors return empty handed, and go out again to sell the last copies. The crowds are excited; the eve of war; opinions clash; passions erupt in the Paris night.*

LUCE.... Si Dreyfus est coupable,—et je le souhaite encore de toutes mes forces—qu'on le prouve, en débats publics: nous nous inclinerons. Mais avant tout, que l'on dissipe cet air irrespirable!

Il s'avance pesamment jusqu'à la fenêtre ouverte, et baigne son regard dans les fraîcheurs vertes du jardin.

Quelques instants passent.

Il se retourne vers Barois, comme s'il se souvenait tout à coup du but de sa convocation; et, familièrement, il lui met ses deux mains sur les épaules.

Cedant arma togæ
(Impression d'audience)

Et on supporte ça!

From the Anti-Dreyfusard *Le Psst!*, 19 February 1898

LUCE.—Barois, j'ai besoin d'un organe où lancer cet appel à la loyauté... (Hésitant) Consentiriez-vous à jeter votre *Semeur* dans la mêlée?

Une telle fierté relève le visage de Barois, que Luce se hâte de parler.

LUCE.—Non, non, écoutez-moi, mon ami. Il faut réfléchir. Voilà deux ans que, pour créer cette revue, vous vous êtes donné, sans restriction. Votre *Semeur* est en plein élan. Eh bien, s'il devient mon porte-voix, tout est compromis; c'est la faillite probable de tous vos efforts...

Barois s'est dressé, trop bouleversé pour répondre. Une joie soudaine, un orgueil immense....

Ils se regardent. Luce a compris. Autour d'eux l'atmosphère s'alourdit. Dans le silence où bat leur double cœur, ils ouvrent les bras et s'étreignent.

C'est le commencement des exaltations surhumaines...

Huit jours plus tard.

Dans la cour de la maison qu'habite Barois, rue Jacob.

Au fond d'une remise ouverte, Woldsmuth et quelques acolytes, sont assis à une table. Breil-Zoeger, Harbaroux, Cresteil, Portal, vont et viennent.

Derrière eux, en piles blanches, 80,000 numéros du *Semeur* sont entassés. Odeur humide de l'impression fraîche.

D'autres ballots, cordés, sont prêts pour la province.

Le long des murs, une centaine de trimardeurs attendent en file indienne, comme à l'entrée d'une soupe populaire.

Trois heures.

La distribution commence.

Barois griffonne des chiffres sur un registre.

Les placards disparaissent, par blocs de 300, sous l'aisselle des coureurs, qui s'enfuient aussitôt vers la rue, sur leurs savates molles.

Déjà les premiers sont hors de la zone où ils doivent se taire, et, boulevard Saint-Germain, rue des Saints-Pères, sur les quais, les cris éclatent: une clameur rauque, dispersée par cent bouches haletantes:

—Numéro spécial!...'LE SEMEUR'!...Révélation sur l'affaire Dreyfus!...'CONSCIENCE', lettre au peuple français, de MARC-

ELIE LUCE, sénateur, membre de l'Institut, professeur au Collège de France...

    Les passants se retournent, s'arrêtent. Les boutiques béent. Des enfants courent. Des mains se tendent.
    Un vent d'orage semble éparpiller les feuilles.
    En deux heures, le vol des papillons blancs s'est abattu jusque dans les quartiers extrêmes, sur la chaussée, sur les tables, au fond des poches.
    Les aboyeurs reviennent, assoiffés, les bras vides.
    La cour s'emplit à nouveau. Le vin coule.
    Les dernières piles sont entamées, épuisées, emportées.
    L'essaim bourdonnant s'échappe une seconde fois, secouant, dans le soir d'été, la torpeur de la ville chaude.
    La foule s'exalte. Les boulevards grouillent.
    Veillée de guerre...
    Déjà, en mille endroits, des pensées françaises, soulevées par cette vague d'héroïsme, s'entrechoquent.
    Une irrésistible explosion de passions a ébranlé le cœur nocturne de Paris.

ROGER MARTIN DU GARD: *Jean Barois* (1st edn. 1913), Nouvelle Revue Française 1917, pp. 204–6.

3. Eulogy: Anatole France

Why did the inveterate sceptic, Anatole France, become a convinced and positive Dreyfusard? Several reasons can be suggested. The crowd was blindly anti-Dreyfusard and Anatole France was cynical of all popular movements: he was inclined to be antigovernment and at first the government refused revision: he desired to be more than a literary figure; and he was influenced by Jaurès into a new faith, socialism. Between 1899 and 1906 he became an ebullient optimist believing in the movement of progress and seeing the Affair as Light against Darkness. Although he had once been highly sceptical of Zola's literature, he came to praise Zola's J'accuse *as a great revolutionary act. By 1908 he had reverted to cynicism, but in 1902 at the funeral of Zola his eloquence was rich and moving. Concluding his speech, he proclaims the birth of a new order of justice due to Zola's action: Zola can be placed among the great men of a great nation: his suffering must be envied; through it he reached unapproachable heights: he was a moment in the conscience of mankind.*

Les conséquences de son acte sont incalculables. Elles se déroulent aujourd'hui avec une force et une majesté puissantes; elles s'étendent indéfiniment: elles ont determiné un mouvement d'équité sociale qui ne s'arrêtera pas. Il en sort un nouvel ordre de choses fondé sur une justice meilleure et sur une connaissance plus profonde des droits de tous.

Messieurs,

Il n'y a qu'un pays au monde dans lequel ces grandes choses pouvaient s'accomplir. Qu'il est admirable le génie de notre patrie! Qu'elle est belle cette âme de la France, qui, dans les siècles passés, enseigna le droit à l'Europe et au monde! La France est le pays de la raison ornée et des pensées bienveillantes, la terre des magistrats équitables et des philosophes humains, la patrie de Turgot, de Montesquieu, de Voltaire et de Malesherbes. Zola a bien mérité de la patrie, en ne désespérant pas de la justice en France.

Ne le plaignons pas d'avoir enduré et souffert. Envions-le. Dressée sur le plus prodigieux amas d'outrages que la sottise, l'ignorance et la méchancété aient jamais élevé, sa gloire atteint une hauteur inaccessible.

Envions-le: il a honoré sa patrie et le monde par une œuvre immense et par un grand acte. Envions-le, sa destinée et son cœur lui firent le sort le plus grand: *Il fut un moment de la conscience humaine.*

ANATOLE FRANCE: *Discours prononcé aux funérailles d'Emile Zola, 5 October 1902.*

4. Ridicule: Georges Sorel

As the philosopher and theorist of Syndicalism—the revolutionary trade-union movement in early twentieth-century France—Sorel would easily have qualified for the extreme wing of the Dreyfusards. In fact, he never took this position, though he was a close friend of Charles Péguy and was a socratic figure at the Left-bank bookshops and cafés where young socialists and idealists met during and after the Affair. What kept him from joining the Dreyfusard cause was a biting scorn for parliamentary democracy, for intellectuals who were qualified by examinations and for the rule of second-rate republicans. He was a rebel with only one cause, his own, though his brilliant mind and scathing wit brought him respect in university circles. His book on the Affair is called The Dreyfusian Revolution *by which he means the transformation of the Republic by new political alignments (see Part Two, chapter 4). Throughout the book he scorns the so-called Dreyfusard heroes.*

*In this passage Zola is lampooned as a man of small mind, posing as a poet and psychologist, a savant and a realist. In fact, Sorel says, he is none of these things, but he deludes the public with his humbug (*boniments*). He is nothing but a clown* ...

Zola a été l'homme représentatif de la bouffonnerie de ces temps. Tout le monde est d'accord pour reconnaître que ce personnage encombrant était un très petit esprit. Il aimait à s'entendre appeler poète, psychologue et savant, sans posséder aucune des qualités qui auraient pu justifier en quoi que ce soit aucun de ces titres: il se donnait comme le chef d'une école réaliste, mais en fait il ne soupçonna jamais ce qui constitue la réalité. Il n'apercevait des choses que de grossiers contours: c'est pourquoi ses admirateurs disent qu'il a surtout réussi dans la description des foules. Sa prétendue violence était toute verbale, il excellait dans l'art d'appeler l'attention du public au moyen de grossiers boniments. On peut le comparer à un clown faisant la parade devant une baraque de foire ...

GEORGES SOREL: *La Révolution Dreyfusienne*, Marcel Rivière, 1909, p. 23.

Part Two
THE AFFAIR AS A CATALYST

I

Nationalist Tensions

The first of the tensions vividly exposed by the Affair has been implicit throughout Part One and because it is the deepest and most pervading it must be treated first. Within it, all other tensions could be placed: it dominates and underlies; its width is the width of modern French history.

The terms 'la patrie', 'la nation', 'le pays', were common coinage on both sides of the Dreyfus debate, but the term 'nationalism' became the property of only one side, that of the anti-Dreyfusards. Of all the terms used to describe an anti-Dreyfusard that of 'nationalist' was the most common, and it was placed in antithesis to the terms Republican or Revolutionary. The antipathy between these concepts would bewilder a student of 1789 who knew nothing of nineteenth-century developments. For the great Revolution was nothing if it was not nationalist. But between the nationalist wars of the Jacobin revolutionaries and the Dreyfus Affair the term 'nationalism' had taken a right-wing, conservative, reactionary connotation. This development is not peculiar to France: it is one of the most interesting European political phenomena of the nineteenth century. But to speak of a revaluation of nationalism from left to right is to play with static terms. In becoming a right-wing attitude nationalism yet retained much of its left-wing ingredients, and it is the new composite which makes nonsense of neat left–right distinctions and makes twentieth-century Fascism so difficult to tabulate. This is already clear during the Affair. Nationalists are in many cases social and political conservatives like Maurras, they draw on the hierarchical, authoritarian tradition of the ancien régime like *La Croix*, and they preach duty, obedience and discipline like Barrès. But the nationalism of Maurras and Barrès is of complex character. If Maurras advocated a return to the old monarchy it was by methods of popular excitement and organisation which were recognisable products of a revolutionary tradition. If Barrès, the great literary nationalist, talked of 'the real nation', *le pays réel*, it was in collectivist terms which owe much to Rousseau. Once the leader of an individualist cult, he came to see virtue in the submission of the individual to the group and community, and the popular element in anti-Dreyfusism was always acceptable to him. This was also true of Jules Lemaître, the first president of the Ligue de la Patrie Française: his nationalism was both élitist and popular at the same time. A regular diner at the salon of Madame de Loynes, he was equally at home in a mass meeting.

In this sense the term 'nationalism' as exposed in the Dreyfus Affair signified more than patriotism: it was more reactionary than conservatism; more radical than republicanism. It looked for a new France based on a charismatic unity of the values of the ancien régime and the vigorous forces of Revolutionary France. Its complexity has often been obscured by Dreyfusard historians who too easily equate it with monarchism or clericalism. Its dynamic appeal to the youth of the prewar generation cannot be explained if these alone were its characteristics.

The antithesis to 'nationalism' during the Dreyfus Affair is less easy to label in one word, but more easy to understand. Gathering together the Revolutionary beliefs in individual rights and justice, the democratic stress on freedom and the socialistic drive towards a new society, the Dreyfusards have often been seen as the upholders of all that is best in the French liberal Revolutionary tradition. Perhaps: but also in Zola, Jean Jaurès the socialist leader, Joseph Reinach the anticlerical publicist and historian of the Affair, Urbain Gohier the antimilitarist, Lucian Herr the socialist librarian of the Left Bank, and Emile Combes, prime minister of the anticlerical government of 1902–5, there are strong elements of all that is *ill*iberal in the Revolutionary tradition: intolerant rationalism, passionate anticlericalism and exclusive republicanism. Like the nationalists they, too, wanted a France in their own image and like the nationalists they, too, were intolerant of deviation and nonconformity. Both sides claimed to be patriotic, both diagnosed treason in the other's campaign: the most belligerent nationalists accused the Jews, Protestants and *métèques*—a word covering all those members of the artificial France, *le pays légal*: their extremist opponents vilified the Jesuits, the clergy, the military hierarchy and the remnants of monarchist families.

This broad division has persisted in the twentieth century. French Fascism of the Action Française in the 1920s and 1930s and of Deat, Doriot and Darnand under Vichy was the activist extreme of the new nationalist spirit, and the hierarchical, authoritarian creeds of Maurras, Colonel de la Rocque, leader of the right wing movement Croix de Feu, and Marshal Pétain, self-appointed saviour of defeated France, perpetuated the emotional attachment to what Barrès called the eternal, predetermined values of *le pays réel*. Pétain and Maurras meeting together at the beginning of Vichy France understood each other perfectly. Alexander Werth used the writing of Réné Benjamin to describe the event.

> The moment the Marshal saw Maurras he rose. Maurras leapt forward, put his hand in the Marshal's, bowed with deep reverence, then smiled radiantly. Their eyes met. They were like two flashes of lightning.... The light of respect. The flame of admiration. The Marshal was saying to himself: 'Here is the best mind that for forty years has been guiding and giving courage to the best men in France' and Maurras wanted to cry out 'Saviour, of magnificent saviour'.

There followed a 'conversation':

> 'What should be taught', said the Marshal forcefully 'is honour.' Maurras closed his eyes in a state of grateful beatitude.
> 'Honour,' he cried, 'that is the most beautiful thing. There is nothing to add to it.'
> 'But it should be defined,' said the Marshal.
> 'A matter of teaching,' said Maurras.
> 'We could start,' said the Marshal with a smile.
> 'I accept, provided I may follow you humbly,' said Maurras entranced.
> ... the whole thing was of course largely an invention—if only because Maurras was stone deaf.[1]

It remains ironic that Maurras should be convicted in 1945 for betraying his country to the Germans; the very crime for which he had execrated Dreyfus. But when he exclaimed at his trial 'This is the revenge of Dreyfus', he was less aware of this irony than of the clear fact that the forces which had brought him to justice represented the

---

[1] Alexander Werth: *France 1940–55*, 1957, p. 66. He is quoting from R. Benjamin: *Le Grand Homme Seul*, 1943.

Revolutionary ideals and tradition which had been exemplified by the Dreyfusards. And certainly the France which both the Popular Front of the 1930s and the Resisters of the 1940s wished to create differed in few respects from that invoked by Clemenceau and Zola, Jaurès and other Dreyfusards.

It is possible to suggest that this clash of ideas over what makes a nation and over what is truly France, is one of the most lasting products of the great Revolution and directly or indirectly of Rousseauist thought. Rousseau, in *Du contrat social*, talked of a 'general will' which in theory united the country. If men could identify their individual wills with the 'general will', then unity and social harmony would be established. English critics of Rousseau have been quick to point out that the 'general will' cannot be measured in any satisfactory way and that the English emphasis on 'majority will' is a more practical basis for a political science. But in France the notion that the country is in theory one, and that the 'general will' is a goal to be attained, has been of continuous influence in post-Revolution political thought. In practice, it had tended to mean that anyone, be he Napoleon, a Republican, a Nationalist or a Resister, who believes he has understood and perceived the 'general will' of France, treats his opponents as enemies not only of himself but of the nation. During the Dreyfus Affair this self-confidence is blatant in many individuals and groups. Drumont and Maurras dismiss Jews and Protestants as artificial Frenchmen, outside the reality of the nation; Zola at his trial sets his view of France and his values against those of the military leaders; Clemenceau declares that Justice is the great French characteristic, and Albert de Mun states in the Chamber that all Frenchmen must stand by the honour of the army.[1] Such examples could be multiplied. The claim of them all is that their vision of France is, or should be, the general one. The conflict is fundamental.

To illustrate this conflict there is the controversy over the army. At the beginning of the Third Republic the relations between army and left-wing politics were based on a unity of attitude: the defence and if possible the revenge of France against the triumphant Germany of 1871. Gambetta, a radical in politics, was a militarist in his respect for the army's rôle in the new Republic. Three major factors removed this good relationship in the period between Gambetta and Dreyfus.

[1] Extracts illustrating these points of view: for Drumont, p. 58, no. 2; for Maurras, p. 41, no. 2; for Zola, p. 38, no. 1; for Clemenceau, p. 34, no. 1; for de Mun, p. 95, no. 1.

Firstly, the politicians grew less interested in *Revanche*, even though the public continued to applaud anyone, like Boulanger, who promised defiance of Germany. Secondly, the army became one of the few areas of status and profession where the right-wing outsiders of the Republic could find employment. Monarchists and Catholics had to a considerable extent been alienated from the Republic by legislation of the late 1870s and early 1880s, and the civil service, like politics, was largely closed to them. The army, however, remained open. Thirdly, the growth of socialist thought and influence introduced an internationalist aspect to French left-wing politics, and with it an attitude which regarded war and militarism as a reactionary class phenomenon. By 1894 the result of these three factors was a tension between the army and certain left-wing parties and personalities. The army, for its supporters, seemed to embody all that was best in French life and tradition; for its opponents it appeared to be, with the church, the last preserve of counter-revolutionary forces.[1]

Out of these tensions, the wide nationalistic one and its microcosm, the conflict over the army, grew the two major Leagues of the Affair. Their essential characteristics are caught in their titles. The Ligue des Droits de l'Homme intentionally recalled the Revolutionary tradition, and the Ligue de la Patrie Française was the embodiment of the new nationalism. In origin the former league was more directly committed to the Affair than the latter. Founded on 20 February 1898 during the Zola trial, the Ligue des Droits de l'Homme expressed the belief that the conviction of Dreyfus, the acquittal of Esterhazy and the proceedings against Zola were not only a travesty of republican justice but also a positive triumph of reaction. The Manifesto of the Intellectuals in *L'Aurore* on 14 January had stated:

> We the undersigned protest against the violation of judicial procedure and against the mystery surrounding the Esterhazy affair and persist in demanding Revision.[2]

The Ligue des Droits de l'Homme continued this demand. By May 1898 it had over 800 adherents and had spread into the provinces, where meetings of republican revivalism were conducted by such men

[1] See Sources, pp. 43-9.
[2] Among the signatures were those of Daniel Halévy, Emile Zola, Marcel Proust, Anatole France (men of letters); Emile Duclaux, Edouard Grimaux (scientists); Claude Monet, Gallé, Carrière (artists); Professors Séailles, Seignobos and Jean Psichari; Léon Blum, Louis Havet, Langevin, Charles Péguy (Sorbonne and other institutions of higher education).

as Emile Durkheim, the sociologist, and Francis de Pressensé, the most ardent of the Ligueurs, a man of Protestant tradition and left-wing politics. By the end of 1898 the League put its membership at over 4,500: it had appealed systematically only to teachers and intellectuals. In theory, it was liberal in its approach to the individual and society; in practice, it became intensely anticlerical, which caused the Catholic Dreyfusard, Paul Viollet, to leave its committee. Where the Ligue des Droits de l'Homme overtly announced its commitment to the Dreyfusard cause, the Ligue de la Patrie Française in December 1898 announced itself as a party of reconciliation: to reconcile in one body all patriots who cared for the interests of the nation. Within this general policy there was room for wide disagreement, and the League always lacked the stability of purpose which its rival had achieved. From the start it claimed to appeal to all sections of the public, and besides the Academicians, the literary figures and the salon habitués who were members in January 1899, it contained 6,000 mechanics from Paris, 3,000 workers from St Etienne and 3,000 from Marseille. By February its membership was 100,000.[1] Its very assertion that it united all patriotic Frenchmen challenged the right of its rivals to represent France. Like the anticlericalism of the Ligue des Droits de l'Homme, this exclusiveness had an intolerance which promised authoritarian measures. The danger of this was apparent to at least one of its more eminent members, Ferdinand Brunetière, who withdrew his name in protest against its Caesarist tendencies.

The refusal of Paul Viollet and Brunetière to conform to the more extreme aspects of their respective leagues points a warning against the division of all participants of the Affair into oversimplified categories. Charles Péguy is another whose ideas were born of a union of apparent opposites. Like Barrès, he was concerned deeply with the national values of France, its people of the soil, its language and customs. But unlike Barrès, Péguy believed that the nation was to be saved not by a return to an old tradition but by the triumph of justice. Poet and idealist, Péguy's Dreyfusism was mystical and elevated. In *Notre Jeunesse* his scorn for the degeneration of the Dreyfusard cause into intolerant

---

[1] Among whom were Paul Bourget, José Maria de Hérédia, de Vogüé, duc de Broglie (Académie Française); Charles Maurras, Jules Verne, Léon Daudet, Pierre Louÿs, Maurice Barrès, Ferdinand Brunetière, François Coppée (men of letters); Henri Vaugeois, Gabriel Syveton, Louis Dausset (higher education); General Cavaignac (whose adherence on 5 January gave it a decidedly anti-Dreyfusard bias).

Allons-y!
(Impression d'audience)

Et on supporte ça!

From the Dreyfusard *Le Sifflet*, 24 February 1898

politics under Combes was passionate and rhetorical.[1] He compared it with the ardour of the early Dreyfusards, with the high ideals of his campaign on the Left Bank as a young socialist and rebel against authority. Since then the nationalist and religious poetry of his last years, and the symbolism of his death at the front in 1914, his face buried in the root crops of a field in provincial France, have given to French nationalism a heroic memory:

> Heureux ceux qui sont morts dans les grandes batailles
> Couchés dessus le sol à la face de Dieu.[2]

Socialist Dreyfusard, Catholic poet, nationalist martyr, Péguy defies simple categorisation. Between the Affair and the First World War he showed that the ideals of the two Leagues could be bridged. Under the pressure of the prewar situation the nationalist tensions in France appeared to be weakened, and in the war it was a Dreyfusard, Georges Clemenceau, who became the symbol of national defiance. But the conflicting visions of France were not reconciled; the fundamental antipathy remained, and its substance must be sought further in the racial, religious and political tensions of the Affair.

SOURCES

The Individual and the Nation

1. Clemenceau

A fiercely eloquent Radical, Clemenceau was the scourge of French political life. Until the Boulanger crisis he was an outspoken critic of the Republic, and although he dropped many of his criticisms in the face of the Boulangist threat, he remained staunchly individualistic. This individualism increased when he was unjustly accused of complicity in the Panama scandal and lost his seat at the next election. He devoted himself to journalism and as editor of L'Aurore *was won to the revisionist cause by a fellow radical Arthur Ranc. In his Dreyfusard writings there is anticlericalism and strong republicanism, but above all a concern for justice which had been denied both to himself and to Dreyfus. In this extract he is confident that justice is the one enduring, indisputable characteristic of republican France, the France of 1789.*

[1] See Sources, p. 123, no. 1, Péguy.
[2] Quoted by Daniel Halévy: *Péguy and Les Cahiers de la Quinzaine*, 1946, p. 223.

He sees the Affair as a symbol, a microcosm of the continuous battle between the innocent victim and the forces of arbitrary tyranny and dogma; in this case the forces of the army and the church. To help the innocent there is one word, small but magical, the concept of justice, and before its power all resistance will fall and the persecuted individual will be justified.

La France en ce moment a l'angoisse de vivre un drame inouï d'humanité. Sans doute l'erreur judiciaire remonte à l'âge du premier homme qui juge, mais vit-on jamais tout un peuple entier, comme les Français de l'heure présente, dans l'action tragique de la justice contre l'iniquité?

Un homme injustement condamné, combien souvent cela s'est-il vu? Combien souvent cela se verra-t-il encore? Les lois violées par ceux-là même, qui en ont la garde, spectacle de tous les jours! Toute la cruauté sociale faisant rage contre la victime, ordinaire effet de la lâcheté anonyme des intérêts au pouvoir! Mais quand, avec le condamné, avec les condamneurs, tout un ordre établi se trouve en cause, quand derrière eux, les grandes forces sociales sont aux prises, quand le droit n'a pour lui que d'être le droit, quand toute l'administration de justice menace ruine en la succession de ses différents organes, quand la conscience individuelle voit se dresser devant elle l'appareil formidable de l'État, soutenu par l'inconscience des foules, alors tout s'agrandit, tout prend des proportions démesurées, et le combat se hausse jusqu'à la légendaire épopée où toute l'humanité comparaît.

La victime, en ce cas, quelque pitié qu'elle inspire, se fond en un vivant symbole de toutes nos défaillances d'esprit et de cœur. Ce représentant passager d'une justice humaine injuste apparaît soudain comme le synthéthique témoin de toutes les iniquités du passé contre toutes les forces de domination sociale qu'une injustice réparée menace d'autres réparations plus redoutables. Il faut que l'injustice représentative demeure, pour que la ligue des puissances maîtresses ne soit pas entamée. La religion de charité brandit le fer et dit 'Malheur au Juif'. L'esprit de caste militaire n'admet pas que la force soit sujette de la raison. Contre la liberté cherchant sa voie se dresse l'autorité du dogme et du fer implacable parce qu'infaillible. L'iniquité *est*: force immense au regard de la justice qui veut être. L'arbitraire s'installe sur la loi, le mensonge sur la vérité, la force écrase la pensée.

Et dans cet effroyable combat de toutes les tyrannies contre la créature désemparée, quel recours pour la débilité d'un seul aux prises avec l'énormité des puissances souveraines? Rien que des idées, des abstractions qui sont néant quand l'homme capable de les concevoir est inapte à les objectiver, à les faire passer de son esprit dans la réalité vivante. Des idées, des mots, mais des mots magiques tout de même comme ces formules des contes d'orient par la vertu desquelles soudainement toute réalité s'abîme dans un éclair de foudre, pour faire place à l'enchantement des féeries.

Justice un bien petit mot. Le plus grand de tous en deçà de la bonté. Prenez le temps où le genre humain courbé sous le plus dur talon, accepte, oublieux de tout, le destin des bêtes passives, choisissez le moment où, désespérant de lui-même il abdique sans regret la dignité de son corps et de son âme pour se ruer aux dégradations des servitudes volontaires, et puis, dans l'effroyable crise d'avilissement qui fait aimer ses chaînes à l'esclave, passez parmi ces hommes stupides de malheur et faites retentir le grand cri: Justice! Justice! C'est assez. Tous ont frémi. Tous sont debout, debout pour la promesse sacrée, tombée miraculeusement des hauteurs, debout pour l'espérance, debout pour la volonté, pour l'effort. Le plus déchu vient de comprendre qu'une heure libératrice sonnait. Le maître a douté de lui-même, et, reconnaissant qu'il n'est rien qu'un homme, prend peur. Un grand frisson d'humanité passe dans l'air. Les cœurs battent. Les mains se cherchent. Une irrésistible impulsion précipite en avant toutes les énergies. Les résistances sont brisées. Une victoire du droit humain s'inscrit en nos annales, jusqu'aux chutes hélas! en des formes nouvelles, que suivront, aux heures fatales, les victoires de l'avenir.

Un beau mot, le mot qui fait des miracles! Un mot que l'homme ne peut entendre sans se trouver plus grand, sans se sentir meilleur. Point de sommeil qu'un tel mot ne rompe, point de mort qui ne soit par lui réveillée. Mot d'ordre des invisibles Dieux qui, par l'éternel appât de justice, entraînent l'homme en leur sillage. Mot plus fort que la force, par l'espérance.

Avec ce mot pour toute arme nous avons engagé la bataille. Par ce mot, toutes les résistances d'oppression, une à une sont tombées. Par ce mot demain le vaincu d'hier tiendra sa légitime revanche.

G. CLEMENCEAU: *L'Iniquité*, Stock, 1899, Préface.

2. Barrès

The anti-Dreyfusism of Barrès was a bitter disappointment to many who, like Lucien Herr and Léon Blum, had been influenced by the vitality and individualism of his early writings. But in many ways it was not inconsistent.

Barrès needed emotional, lyrical stimulus, and he hated the rational, positivist, logical intellectuals of his time. He was moved by Boulangism and he was captured by the emotional patriotism of the crowds who vilified Dreyfus. During the Affair he reviled the intellectuals among the revisionists as a subversive force undermining the emotional vigour of the nation by their rationalism. At Rennes in this report he saw the question purely in terms of national interests, although the appearance of Dreyfus moved him to some initial pity. The prisoner was clearly a traitor, but the real criminals, he continues, are the intellectuals who have tried to twist the nation to their own image. Against these men he exalts the loyalty of the generals. The conflict between the army and the internal enemies of France will be a racial struggle. By implication the Dreyfusards are not all true Frenchmen.

La justice et l'Etat sont satisfaits. — La moralité publique et le salut national voulaient, contre le gouvernement, la condamnation d'un traître utilisé par une faction. Il ne s'agit pas d'avoir des idées 'généreuses'; il s'agit d'avoir des idées raisonnables. Ah! c'est toujours plus *agréable* d'absoudre que de condamner. C'est toujours commode de détourner ses yeux et de dire: 'Pauvre diable!'

... Pour moi, je l'ai souvent répété, j'avais une opinion dans l'affaire Dreyfus, avant de connaître les faits judiciaires. Je me rangeais à l'opinion des hommes que la société a désignés pour être compétents. Je suis allé à Rennes surtout avec le sentiment de l'intérêt public. Ainsi je ne m'y rendais pas avec une âme sans passion. Pourtant, la présence réelle de Dreyfus m'a tout d'abord amolli. Je l'ai plaint. Et si j'avais, dans cette loque humaine, senti un innocent, je me serais retiré de la lutte. Il n'est pas beau d'être le combattant qui passe d'une armée dans l'autre; peut-être me serais-je borné à me taire, après deux mots d'explication; jamais je n'aurais aidé à sceller sur un innocent la pierre d'infamie. Mais j'ai vu, au cours de ces longues audiences, la figure de Dreyfus suer la trahison.

J'ai dit, au bout de quinze jours, à mes lecteurs: 'La condamnation est certaine.' Avais-je donc un renseignement? Les juges n'ont parlé à personne. Je les connaissais comme des Français, et je voyais le crime assis devant eux.

Réjouissons-nous en toute liberté d'esprit. La France vient d'être servie.

Et si la peine de Dreyfus est allégée, nous pouvons prendre de cela aussi de la satisfaction. C'est une bête humaine, qui respire et qui souffre. Son pire crime, d'ailleurs, n'est pas d'avoir livré les documents énumérés au bordereau, c'est d'avoir servi pendant cinq ans à ébranler l'armée et la nation totale. Or, de cette campagne antifrançaise menée depuis 1894, il est le moyen plutôt que l'inspirateur.

Les grands responsables, que le châtiment devrait atteindre, ce sont les 'intellectuels', les 'anarchistes de l'estrade', les 'métaphysiciens de la sociologie'. Une bande de fous d'orgueil. Des gens qui ont en leur intelligence une complaisance criminelle, qui traitent d'idiots nos généraux, d'absurdes nos institutions sociales et de malsaines nos traditions. Ces pédants révoltés sont en même temps les plus inféconds des hommes. S'il y a des abus et des faiblesses dans notre état-major, s'il y a des parties pourries dans notre société, s'il y a des préjugés à émonder de nos traditions nationales, cette œuvre de revision doit être entreprise dans un sentiment d'amour, avec l'esprit d'un père de famille qui gère les intérêts des siens, et non avec l'audace de ces pédants et artistes néroniens qui s'écrient: 'Périsse un ordre social qui ne veut pas se plier sur l'idéal que je me suis composé!'

... Ne nous souvenons plus du traître que pour aimer ceux qui le châtièrent. Exprimons notre reconnaissance à ces officiers, les Mercier, les Roget, les Deloye, environnés désormais d'une immense popularité, qui nous donnèrent de magnifiques exemples de claire raison française. Confions-nous à cette jeune armée, dont nous vîmes les représentants gravir les marches de l'estrade au lycée de Rennes. Ils ont resserré et justifié la fraternité française.

Conséquence terrible pour certains: la question de races est ouverte.

Il y a une conscience nationale: c'est l'entente de gens qui sont réunis depuis plusieurs générations dans les mêmes institutions sociales pour affirmer des intérêts moraux communs.

La conscience nationale française a été irritée, froissée, parce que des étrangers de l'intérieur et de l'extérieur ont voulu nous 'faire marcher'. Nous enregistrons avec une immense espérance la victoire de Rennes!

M. BARRÈS: *Scènes et Doctrines du Nationalisme*, Plon, 1902, vol. I, pp. 208–10.

Two French Prophets

1. Zola

During the Affair the 'scientific' novelist Emile Zola posed as the great clairvoyant. But despite his scientific claims, he acted out of belief and personal conviction rather than objective proof. Dreyfusism was a cause worthy of a man who had already shocked the army with his book on the Franco-Prussian war, La Débâcle, *and the Catholics with his critical treatment of Lourdes and Rome. He came to see the Affair as Good against Evil, Truth against Error, and prophesied that Dreyfusism would become the new religion of democracy. In his speech at his trial he indulged in this prophetic rhetoric at the expense of the army leaders. The France of the Revolution he declares is threatened by the injustice, the obscurity, the error of the Affair. The future of France is at stake. It could be isolated in the world by its own blindness. The truth must be spoken, and Zola is there to speak it. In a flamboyant conclusion he swears to the innocence of Dreyfus on the reputation of his writing. He is prepared to gamble his life and honour: one day France will be grateful.*

L'affaire Dreyfus, ah! Messieurs, elle est devenue bien petite à l'heure actuelle, elle est bien lointaine, devant les terrifiantes questions qu'elle a soulevées. Il n'y a plus d'affaire Dreyfus, il s'agit désormais de savoir si la France est encore la France des Droits de l'Homme, celle qui a donné la liberté au monde et qui devait lui donner la justice. Sommes-nous encore le peuple le plus noble, le plus fraternel, le plus généreux? Allons-nous garder en Europe notre renom d'équité et d'humanité? Puis, ne sont-ce pas toutes les conquêtes que nous avions faites et qui sont remises en question? Ouvrez les yeux, et comprenez que, pour être dans un tel désarroi, l'âme française doit être remuée jusque dans ses intimes profondeurs, en face d'un péril redoutable. Un peuple n'est point bouleversé de la sorte, sans que sa vie morale elle-même soit en danger. L'heure est d'une gravité exceptionnelle, il s'agit du salut de la nation.

Et, quand vous aurez compris cela, Messieurs, vous sentirez qu'il n'est qu'un seul remède possible: dire la vérité, rendre la justice. Tout ce qui retardera la lumière, tout ce qui ajoutera des ténèbres aux ténèbres, ne fera que prolonger et aggraver la crise. Le rôle des bons citoyens, de ceux qui sentent l'impérieux besoin d'en finir, est d'exiger le grand jour. Nous sommes déjà beaucoup à le penser. Les hommes de littérature, de philosophie et de science se lèvent de toutes parts, au nom de l'intelligence et de la raison. Et je ne vous parle pas de l'étranger, du frisson qui a gagné l'Europe tout entière. Pourtant, l'étranger n'est pas forcément l'ennemi. Ne parlons pas des peuples qui peuvent être demain des adversaires. Mais la grande Russie, notre alliée, mais la petite et généreuse Hollande, mais tous les peuples sympathiques du Nord, mais ces terres de langue française, la Suisse et la Belgique, pourquoi donc ont-elles le cœur si gros, si débordant de fraternelle souffrance? Rêvez-vous une France isolée dans le monde? Voulez-vous, quand vous passerez la frontière, qu'on ne sourie plus à votre bon renom légendaire d'équité et d'humanité?

Hélas! Messieurs, ainsi que tant d'autres, vous attendez peut-être le coup de foudre, la preuve de l'innocence de Dreyfus, qui descendrait du ciel comme un tonnerre. La vérité ne procède pas ainsi d'habitude, elle demande quelque recherche et quelque intelligence. La preuve! Nous savons bien où elle est, où l'on pourrait la trouver. Mais nous ne songeons à cela que dans le secret de nos âmes, et notre angoisse patriotique est qu'on se soit exposé l'honneur de l'armée dans un mensonge. Je veux aussi déclarer nettement que, si nous avons notifié comme témoins certains membres des ambassades, notre volonté formelle était à l'avance de ne pas les citer ici. On a souri de notre audace. Je ne crois pas qu'on en ait souri au ministère des Affaires étrangères, car là, on a dû comprendre. Nous avons simplement voulu dire à ceux qui savent toute la vérité que nous la savons, nous aussi. Cette vérité court les ambassades, elle sera demain connue de tous. Et, s'il nous est impossible d'aller dès maintenant la chercher où elle est, protégée par d'infranchissables formalités, le Gouvernement qui n'ignore rien, le Gouvernement qui est convaincu comme nous de l'innocence de Dreyfus (*vives protestations*) pourra, quand il le voudra, et sans risques, trouver les témoins qui feront enfin la lumière.

Dreyfus est innocent, je le jure! J'y engage ma vie, j'y engage mon honneur. A cette heure solennelle, devant ce tribunal qui représente la justice humaine, devant vous, Messieurs les jurés, qui êtes l'incarnation même du pays, devant toute la France, devant le monde entier, je jure que Dreyfus est innocent! Et, par tout ce que j'ai conquis, par le nom que je me suis fait, par mes œuvres qui ont aidé à l'expansion des lettres françaises, je jure que Dreyfus est innocent! Que tout cela croule, que mes œuvres périssent, si Dreyfus n'est pas innocent! Il est innocent!

Tout semble être contre moi: les deux Chambres, le pouvoir civil, le pouvoir militaire, les journaux à grand tirage, l'opinion publique qu'ils ont empoisonnée. Et je n'ai pour moi que l'idée, un idéal de vérité et de justice. Et je suis bien tranquille, je vaincrai.

Je n'ai pas voulu que mon pays restât dans le mensonge et dans l'injustice. On peut me frapper ici. Un jour, la France me remerciera d'avoir aidé à sauver son honneur.

(*Des murmures se font entendre chaque fois que M. Emile Zola répète:*

'*Je jure que Dreyfus est innocent!*' On crie: '*La preuve! la preuve! Donnez la preuve!*')

E. ZOLA, 21 February 1898: in Louis Leblois, *L'Affaire Dreyfus: l'iniquité, la réparation*, Quillet, 1929, pp. 678–9.

2. Maurras

Before the Affair Charles Maurras was not widely known, but in one long article after Colonel Henry's suicide he became the spokesman of the anti-Dreyfusards and later the leader of monarchist revivalism (see chapter 4). Although cold and clinical in his approach to every problem, he could write with passion and fanaticism. More dogmatic than Barrès, he came to supplant him as prophet of nationalism. His justification of Henry's forgeries is one of the most powerful pieces of polemic during the Affair. In the first part he argued that Henry had not really invented anything; he had reproduced documents which actually existed but could not be made public for security reasons. In any case the question of forgery was immaterial. Henry, he stated, had been patriotic and had surrendered his life for his country. In the second part he promises that Henry's sacrifice shall be recognised. The nation will one day come to its senses. Henry's achievements were ones of skill, courage and independence. With his cry of '*Allons-y*' he had led the way. In the end he will be remembered. Statues will be built: the nation will be grateful.

LE PREMIER SANG. II

... Colonel votre sang qui ruissela jusqu'au milieu de la cellule depuis le lit de camp où vous vous étiez étendu, a été, disent les journaux, soigneusement épongé par les ordres du commandant du Mont Valérien. Mais c'est là une grande erreur. Sachez que de ce sang précieux, le premier sang français versé dans l'Affaire Dreyfus, il n'est pas une seule goutte qui ne fume encore, partout où palpite le cœur de la nation. Ce sang fume et criera jusqu'à ce que l'effusion en soit expiée non pas par vous qui avez cédé à de beaux désespoirs, non pas même par la fâcheuse côterie ministérielle de Cavaignac, mais bien par vos premiers bourreaux, je les désigne, par les membres du syndicat de la trahison.

Dans l'état de désordre où sont les partis nationaux, nous n'avons pu vous faire les grandes funérailles dues à votre martyre. Il fallait secouer sur nos boulevards la tunique sanglante et les lames souillées promener le cercueil, arborer le drap mortuaire en manière de drapeau noir. Ce sera notre honte de ne l'avoir point essayé, mais le sentiment national bien que dispersé et divisé contre lui-même, encore incapable d'action, n'en est pas moins ressuscité. Attendez, colonel, qu'il se réveille et se reforme. Accordez-lui quelque crédit. Il vaincra et vous vengera. Avant peu de temps sortiront du sol de la patrie, dans Paris, dans votre village, les monuments expiatoires de notre lâcheté. On y attestera quelle personne vraiment humaine vous avez été parmi nous.

Force, décision, finesse, rien ne vous a manqué sauf un peu de bonheur sur votre dernier jour. Cet insuccès né du hasard ne fera oublier ni votre intelligence ni votre caractère, ni cet audacieux esprit d'entreprise ni cette subtilité un peu retorse de votre pensée qui vous désignaient pour le service que vous remplissiez. Vous vous êtes conduit dans les plus difficiles moments avec suite et indépendance, avec un sentiment de la responsabilité devenu si rare chez nous que l'on en a fait le lot des Anglo-Saxons. Vous que l'on nous dépeint comme une brute à baïonnette, simple esclave de la consigne mal comprise et du devoir mal entendu, comme un malheureux factionnaire arrivé par des protections inespérées à des dignités éminentes, vous avez déployé en toute circonstance, tant à votre bureau de renseignements qu'à la cour d'assises, où chacun admirait la bonhomie et l'énergie de votre allure, des dons supérieurs d'initiative et de résolution. Vous les avez employés avec frénésie jusqu'à tromper vos chefs, vos amis, vos collègues, vos compatriotes pour le bien et l'honneur de tous. Votre mot d'‘ALLONS-Y’ qui passait en proverbe prend désormais une mystérieuse et profonde signification. Cela reste un mot de soldat, et cela devient encore un mot de moraliste et d'homme d'État. Nous ferons qu'il soit immortel et contienne comme une tombe votre mémoire.

Nous pourrions vous louer soit de votre *self same*, soit d'avoir été *the right man in the right place* bien que le *Temps*, blâmé à cet égard par M. Ranc ait contesté le dernier point. Nous userons de préférence d'un vocabulaire français. En toute occasion nous disons que dans la vie comme dans la mort *vous êtes allé en avant*. Vos anciens adversaires publient partout que vous y avez trébuché: ils ne le disons pas toujours. S'il faut en croire de beaux vers:

> '... Le chantre divin tombe et se précipite
> Jusques au plus bas lieu pour gagner les sommets.'

Les héros ont parfois cette destinée des poètes. Que (chose incroyable et honteuse) un *revision* vénale et sommaire vienne vous infliger quelques chutes posthumes, nous demanderons *la revision de la revision mensongère*: ce sera cette fois une agitation moins intéressée mais plus intéressante que les campagnes favorables à l'odieux Dreyfus. L'esprit public bien évadé de la servitude anarchiste, rendre Dreyfus au bagne et vous dédiera des statues. Votre 'faux' malheureux sera compté entre vos meilleurs faits de guerre, tout ce qu'il eut de déplorable, son insuccès, ayant été payé et surpayé de votre sang.

Comptez sur les Français mon colonel pour faire rembourser à votre mémoire ce surplus d'un sang généreux.

CHARLES MAURRAS: *La Gazette de France*, 7 September 1898.

The Rôle of the Army

1. Gohier

An exmonarchist and an antisemite, Urbain Gohier was also the most notorious of the antimilitarists during the Affair. After J'accuse, many revisionists, including Clemenceau, Jaurès and Reinach, attacked the army leaders for injustice and incompetence, but none went to the extremes of Gohier. In this, one of his most violent denunciations, written with colour and passion, he shows the personal fanaticism which finally alienated him from most of the Dreyfusards. He argues that the Affair is only an incident in the struggle between democracy and the counter-revolution. While the power of the army remains the Revolution is unfinished. Monarchists and Catholics are using the army in their plot against the Republic. Military oppression is spreading, displayed in festivals and art. Against this persecution there is only one solution: to defy openly and, if necessary, by force every move of the militarists: to shoot before being shot, literally. If only Napoleon had been assassinated ...

Contre la nation l'armée se lève ou menace de se lever.

Les éternels ennemis du peuple et de la Patrie, les internationaux de Coblentz et les internationaux de Rome, appuyés par les internationaux de la finance, ont tramé ce complot détestable et conçu cet audacieux espoir: de lancer sur la nation l'armée nationale.

Follement, la démocratie à peine affranchie a livré ses enfants à la faction cléricale et ses soldats à la faction féodale. Elle peut en mourir demain.

Au milieu des graves événements qui s'accomplissent ou qui se préparent, l'Affaire Dreyfus n'est qu'un incident. Elle a tiré au jour les arcanes du pouvoir militaire; elle a révélé ce qu'on ignorait, confirmé ce qu'on soupçonnait de sa corruption, de ses méfaits, de ses desseins criminels. Mais elle n'a pas créé la crise; tout au plus l'a-t-elle compliquée. Le mal couvait; il se fût déclaré à tout autre occasion.

...Il est ridicule d'imaginer que la lutte où nous échangeons des coups vient d'éclater. Il y a plus de cent ans que la Révolution et la contre-Révolution sont aux prises, avec des fortunes diverses. Jusqu'ici nulle victoire définitive. Souvent terrassée, jamais écrasée, la contre-Révolution croit tenir aujourd'hui sa revanche. Elle dresse déjà ses listes de proscriptions, nomme ses cours prévôtales et ses exécuteurs, pour la saignée qu'elle pratique dans le peuple environ tous les vingt-cinq ans.

Nos glorieux pères et grand-pères ont cru deux ou trois fois qu'ils avaient consommé la Révolution. Toujours ils l'ont manquée.

L'ancien régime subsiste à peu près intact, sous un décor différent A la place de la pauvre Bastille abattue, vingt Bastilles, cent Bastilles se dressent, plus redoutables. La liberté, la fortune, la vie, l'honneur des citoyens sont à la merci des fantaisies administratives, policières, judiciaires, militaires... La Révolution n'est pas à refaire; elle n'a pas été faite: elle est à faire.

...Les gens de Coblentz et de Rome ne se sont pas donné la peine de restaurer la monarchie pour remettre la nation sous le joug. Ils se sont emparés de la République. Avant tout ils tiennent l'armée... et par les trois millions de citoyens, au moins par les quatre cent mille jeunes soldats sur lesquels la démocratie stupide leur a donné droit de vie et de mort ils terrorisent le peuple.

...La sédition s'était étalée déjà brutalement au cours du procès Zola. Durant les deux semaines infâmes de février 1898, on avait vu le palais de justice pris d'assaut, le jury à plat ventre sous la Botte, la ferraille des sabres traînant sur les dalles, les commencements d'assassinats, les témoins outragés, la tourbe césarienne vomissant l'injure et la menace, les généraux récitant avec effronterie leurs gros mensonges puérils et tous les fuyards, les capitulards de la défense nationale, l'échine encore bleue des coups de bâton de l'étranger, brûlant de prendre pour la seconde fois une sanglante revanche sur le peuple qui les paye.

...Le 21 janvier avant le procès j'avais dit dans l'*Aurore* 'Il s'agit de savoir si la nation matera la sédition du pouvoir militaire ou si le pouvoir militaire courbera définitivement la nation sous le joug'. Le 4 mars après le procès *Le Figaro* concluait 'La société militaire et la société civile sont aux prises; la lutte se terminera dans un nombre quelconque d'années par la domestication et la soumission de l'une des deux rivales'.

... A mesure que l'effroi de la guerre augmente le charlatanisme chauvin s'étale plus effrontément. La parade du 14 juillet, le moindre défilé de polytechniciens ou de pompiers déchaîne un délire belliqueux. ... On frappe des médailles commémoratives de la Débâcle; on élève dans tous les coins des statues aux généraux de déroute ou de reddition. Les livres pour les hommes, les tableaux des expositions regorgent d'allemands et d'anglais défaits, prisonniers, abattus aux pieds du soldat français et demandant grâce. La peinture à l'huile et la peinture à l'eau nous assurent d'innombrables victoires que chantent les pitres du café-concert. Patriotisme et pornographie, pièces à femmes et pièces à soldats se disputent le théâtre.

... Telle étant la situation qu'y a-t-il à faire? Qu'y a-t-il à faire pour cette poignée d'hommes libres qui sont noyés dans la multitude servile—qui luttent perpétuellement pour la raison, pour la justice, pour la vérité contre une immense majorité d'ignorants, de fanatiques, d'insensés—qui de tout temps essuyèrent en France la persécution— mais qui pourtant donnent au monde l'illusion d'une France généreuse et noble?

... Il faut dire: *Nous ne voulons pas*. Que le peuple soit prêt à la servitude ou même qu'il l'appelle de ses vœux, nous entendons qu'il reste libre. Pour ne pas être entraînés dans son esclavage, nous le retiendrons dans la liberté. Nous le forcerons d'être libre, non pour lui, mais pour nous.

Nous ne sommes guère? C'est vrai. Mais de l'autre côté les meneurs ne sont pas beaucoup non plus. La masse nous verrait écrasés avec plaisir, avec une joie envieuse: mais elle est trop lâche, et trop occupée ailleurs pour nous écraser d'elle-même. Elle est inerte. Il faut seulement empêcher qu'on ne l'échauffe, qu'on ne la mette en action. Qu'on arrête à temps les piqueurs et les valets de chiens: la meute ne quittera pas le chevil.

Combien cela fait-il de monde? Dix mille officiers, à peine, sur le double; vingt-cinq mille hommes en tout, conduits par deux à trois cents chefs. Il y a en France plus de vingt-cinq mille hommes résolus à prévenir le mauvais coup: il y a plus de trois cents hommes qui seraient d'abord fusillés ou déportés en Guyane par le dictateur et sa bande. C'est un cas de légitime défense. Dès qu'on fera mine de nous mettre en joue, tirons les premiers. Sans métaphore.

Des sociétés naïves se fondent pour 'défendre' les droits de l'homme et du citoyen par la concorde universelle. Quelle ingénuité! Défense suppose combat. L'homme qui braque une arme sur ma poitrine, je le tue.

... Le 1er mars 1815 comme Napoléon débarquait de l'Île d'Elbe à Cannes pour mettre encore l'Europe à feu et à sang, le maire d'un village voisin lui dit 'Nous commencions à être heureux et tranquilles; vous allez tout troubler'. Si ce magistrat municipal, au lieu de discourir avait envoyé au Corse une balle dans le ventre, il eût sauvé de la mort plus de cinquante mille hommes, il eût sauvé la France d'une seconde invasion, du démembrement, de l'occupation étrangère. Ni plus ni moins.

U. GOHIER: *L'Armée contre la Nation*, Editions de la Revue Blanche, 1898, pp. v–xxxiii.

2. Brunetière

Ferdinand Brunetière was a distinguished literary historian and critic and a professor of French literature and language. According to many, his university environment should have made him a Dreyfusard. But he had attacked the naturalism in Zola's literature, which ran counter to his ideas of the moral purpose of art, and he looked for order and discipline in society. There were many anti-Dreyfusards who defended the army more passionately than Brunetière, just as there were Dreyfusards who attacked it more moderately than Gohier. This article attempts to explode the charge that the army was an undemocratic force, and as such it is one answer to Gohier's invective. He claims for the army several functions: it protects the country, it unites the nation, it brings equality of experience, it disciplines and it counterbalances the power of money. In an age of growing materialism it encourages loyalty, self-sacrifice and honest impartiality.

Nous voulons donc et il nous faut une Armée—premièrement, parce que nous voulons messieurs continuer d'être la France, et qu'une Armée est l'instrument ou l'organe nécessaire de protection, de défense, et d'action de cette personne historique et morale qui s'appelle la France.

... Nous voulons en second lieu, une armée et il nous en faut une— parce que nous voulons continuer d'être une nation, une Nation et non pas une société d'assurances, une juxtaposition, un syndicat, un agrégat d'intérêts. Nous voulons une Armée parce que nous sommes et nous voulons continuer d'être un organisme vivant, dont toutes les parties se tiennent ou se répondent un véritable organisme.... Dans une démocratie c'est l'Armée nationale qui relie pour ainsi dire à leur centre les extrémités du territoire commun et qui du centre à ces extrémités communique et propage la pulsation de la vie. Car, quelle autre institution voyez-vous qui pût jouer ce rôle? Ce n'est pas la magistrature, qui n'est qu'une aristocratie, une élite, un état-major sans soldats. Ce ne sont pas les universités dont la tendance, que j'approuve, est d'être ou de devenir de plus en plus 'régionales'. Mais c'est bien l'Armée, l'Armée seule, l'Armée nationale, l'Armée recrutée de tous les points de territoire, dans toutes les classes de la société, l'Armée reproduisant dans sa hiérarchie l'image de cette société; l'Armée enfin analogue ou conforme, dans son organisation comme dans son esprit à la démocratie dont elle émane et j'ajoute messieurs, l'Armée rappelant pour ainsi dire, de génération en génération la démocratie à son principe essentiel.

C'est en effet une troisième raison pour laquelle nous voulons et pour laquelle il nous faut une Armée ... parce que nous sommes une démocratie et parce que ... nous croyons, nous messieurs, qu'entre une démocratie et une Armée nationale il y a des rapports, des convenances, des affinités profondes.... Une armée nationale abaisse ceux qui sont en haut; elle élève ceux qui sont en bas: que voulez-vous de plus démocratique?

... Pour moi j'aime l'armée d'être la grande 'Niveleuse'. Oui, je l'aime pour la régularité fonctionnelle avec laquelle elle ramène les générations au sentiment de l'égalité. Français du Nord et Français du Midi, paysans, ouvriers, bourgeois, aristocrates, intellectuels, elle les mêle tous ensemble, et tous ensemble elle les soumet à l'action de la même discipline.

... Nous voulons encore et il nous faut une Armée: parce qu'en France, et surtout dans le siècle où nous sommes, après tant d'agitations et de révolutions, nous éprouvons le besoin de quelque discipline.... La discipline au fond c'est l'éducation de la sensibilité: c'est la formation du caractère et de la volonté; c'est l'apprentissage de la solidarité; c'est la réunion des moyens qui, en temps de paix comme en temps de guerre ont pour objet d'assurer et d'augmenter le 'rendement moral' de l'individu.

Il n'est pas ici question de savoir si la discipline militaire a toujours cet effet; il suffit qu'elle devrait l'avoir; et quand elle ne l'a pas, les moyens peuvent être défectueux puisqu'ils sont humains, mais tel est bien son idéal; et on le retrouverait dans l'esprit de toutes les institutions militaires.

Je dis en outre qu'elle seule est capable de le réaliser. Et, en effet, tandis que toutes les autres formes de l'action nous enseignent la concurrence pour la vie et travaillent plus ou moins à l'émancipation de l'individu, celle-ci seule nous apprend l'union pour la victoire.

... Et nous voulons enfin et il nous faut une Armée—pour que dans une société comme la nôtre il y ait quelque chose au moins qui contrebalance le pouvoir de l'argent. C'est ici Messieurs que je fais appel aux socialistes avec la sympathie d'un homme qui est d'ailleurs assez éloigné de partager toutes leurs idées, mais qui du moins a ceci de commun avec eux de ne vivre que de son travail. Suis-je 'une classe dirigeante'? Je n'en sais rien; mais ce que je sais bien c'est que j'ai, sinon la haine—je ne veux pas user de paroles violentes—mais la défiance instinctive et invincible de la ploutocratie. Et je dis, à ceux de nos socialistes qui s'exaltent, pour ainsi parler, dans la défiance de l'institution militaire, je leur fais observer que le terme nécessaire, inévitable et dernier de cette politique 'économique', financière, industrielle, commerciale, vers laquelle on les pousse, c'est justement la ploutocratie. Vous accusez l'Armée comme on dit dans vos congrès, d'être l'instrument du capitalisme; et non seulement elle ne l'est point, mais c'est elle qui en limite au contraire les excès et, dans un temps comme le nôtre c'est elle contre la tyrannie matérialiste de l'argent, qui demeure notre principale et presque notre unique sauvegarde.

Si nous écoutons en effet les voix qui nous viennent aujourd'hui de toutes parts, voix de la finance, voix du commerce et de l'industrie, voix de la science même quelquefois, que nous disent-elles? 'Enrichistoi, voilà le vrai but de ton activité et le grand objet de ta vie! N'aie d'égard qu'à la fortune, sans trop te soucier des moyens par lesquels on l'acquiert, et demeure persuadé que les millions sentent toujours bon.' Mais une voix répond 'N'en croyez rien, ô jeunes gens! Usez de l'argent comme n'en usant pas. Ne sacrifiez à la fortune aucune de vos naturelles fiertés, ni une parcelle de votre indépendance! Gardez toujours vos mains pures. Faites-vous une religion de l'honneur et un culte de désintéressement. Ne méprisez pas les riches, ils n'ont pas tous fait exprès de l'être, et ne condamnez pas la richesse, elle peut avoir son utilité. Mais ne vous inclinez pas! ne pliez jamais le genou devant elle! et soyez, s'il le faut, orgueilleux de votre pauvreté.' C'est, Messieurs, ce que la voix de l'armée nous dit éloquemment; et Dieu veuille que notre démocratie ne cesse pas de l'entendre, s'il y va non seulement de sa dignité, mais de son existence même!

F. BRUNETIÈRE: *La Nation et l'Armée*, Bureaux de 'la Patrie Française', 26 April 1899, pp. 12–22.

II
Racial Tensions

It is interesting to ask the question 'Would there have been a Dreyfus Affair if Dreyfus had not been a Jew?' Of course it could be argued that this is not an historical question and that no answer is possible. But many contemporaries of the Affair gave what amounts to a clear answer. Certain Dreyfusards, particularly conscious of Dreyfus as a Jew, stated that his arrest and conviction were a direct attack on the whole Jewish race; a racialism planned and executed with the intention of driving the Jews from their social positions or even from the country. On the anti-Dreyfusard side most antisemites asserted that Dreyfus was a traitor because he was a Jew: he could be nothing else. Both attitudes implied that if Dreyfus had not been a Jew the Affair would never have materialised, either (from the first attitude) because he would not have been arrested and certainly not convicted, or (from the second attitude) because he would never have betrayed his country. Thus by asking what seems to be an unhistorical question one arrives at an historical conclusion: the Jewishness of Dreyfus was seen to be fundamental; the *sine qua non* of the Affair. This is not to say that all the participants of the Affair were either Jewish apologists or antisemites. Picquart was a Dreyfusard but no friend of the Jews, Brunetière was a nationalist but no antisemite; Scheurer-Kestner never became involved in Jewish apologetics. But unprejudiced as they may have been, they took part in what Péguy has called 'the Great Crisis of Israel'.

Antisemitism in France as in other European countries stretches back into the middle ages. The sectarianism of the Jews, their historical antipathy to Christianity and their internationalism has set them apart from national Christian societies, and this estrangement has been aggravated to a point of tension by the periodic need of these societies to find a scapegoat for personal, economic or national disasters. However assimilated in theory, the Jew has always been a potential, if not an actual, outsider. (This is an historical statement which does not imply a moral imperative.) The racialism which polluted the Affair was a product of both these interconnected factors in the particular setting of the early Third Republic.

The first factor can be examined by asking 'How far did the Jews stress their differences from the rest of French society?' Undoubtedly a small number were conscious of their race and religion to a point of exclusiveness. In 1897 Bernard Lazare declared at a Jewish meeting that a common past of persecution, common customs, literature and philosophy, all combined to make the Jews a real nation:

> Moreover it is because they are a nation that antisemitism exists... and what are the effects of this antisemitism? To make this nationality more tangible for the Jews, to strengthen their realisation that they are a people.[1]

Similarly, the Jewish paper *L'Univers Israélite* called, during the Affair, for a consolidation of the Jews to defeat their racial and social opponents, and this assertiveness was buttressed by the eloquence of Alexander Weill, the Jewish poet, and Zadoc Kahn, the Grand Rabbi of France, who both reacted strongly to the antisemitism of Drumont.

Their protests, it might be held, increased the antisemitic tendencies in France and led to a wider belief that a Jewish syndicate plotting treason against the French nation really existed. But Lazare, especially, was something of a prophet, calling his people to self-consciousness. As he admits, the vast majority of the French Jews wished only to live in assimilated harmony with the rest of France.

> The Jews of France... are themselves the best agents of antisemitism. Instead of reacting against their enemies they persist—with rare exceptions—in developing their cowardice and passive acceptance of evil. They sanction the policy of silence and wait on events.[2]

L'Univers Israélite made the same criticisms, and Charles Péguy in *Notre Jeunesse* wrote:

> The great majority of Jews... fear conflict: they fear trouble. They fear unrest: more than anything perhaps, they fear, they distrust simple inconvenience. They prefer silence, servile calm.[3]

The passivity they criticised was the average Jew's reaction to both antisemitism and the Affair. His interests, he believed, lay in assimilation. The antisemite's accusation that the Affair was a vast Jewish plot cannot be substantiated. Apart from one or two Jewish writers and leaders, the French Jews did not openly vaunt their racial and

[1] Bernard Lazare: *Le nationalisme juif*, 6 March 1897.   [2] Ibid.
[3] Charles Péguy: *Notre Jeunesse*, 1933 edn., p. 68.

religious exclusiveness. But if their expression was muted, did their positions in society amount to Jewish assertiveness? A multitude of articles in the 1880s and 1890s compared the Jewish achievements and positions in France with their numerical strength and reached the conclusion that their influence was totally out of proportion to their size. Although the figures they quoted were mostly fictitious, these articles had some grounding in fact. If one chose to emphasise race it was true that Jews were prominent in certain occupations, especially in the theatre, journalism, literature, law, medicine and politics. It is an established psycho-sociological generalisation that a minority prone to persecution tends to exert itself with greater determination than the majority, which is secure in its traditional, numerical strength. But to emphasise the social and economic success of the Jews would be to forget that a large number of them were members of the proletariat. In Paris, where there were some 45,000 Jews, the number of Jewish workers has been estimated at 20,000.[1] Jews did not form a homogeneous class, and because of this their economic and social interests were diffuse.

In assessing the first factor in racial tension one can reach an initial conclusion: the passivity and social diffusion of the Jews makes it impossible to talk meaningfully of a united Jewish society or a concerted Jewish attitude. But at the time of the Affair those with a tendency to antisemitism were not so analytic. They focused on the Jews who were prominent in society, on those like the Rothschilds who were of international significance and on those Jewish writers who saw their race and religion in positive terms and who were prepared to meet racial prejudice with racial assertion.

But the provocative status or expression of certain Jews, however exaggerated by their opponents, is not sufficient to explain antisemitism. One must turn to the other factor producing racialism and ask, 'Who were the antisemites and what accounts for the intensive outburst of prejudice before and during the Affair?' For any adequate answer one needs not only a detailed political and sociological analysis but also a number of biographies. What, for example, made the artist Dégas an antisemite? How was Urbain Gohier able to combine antimilitarism with rabid antisemitism? And what is the origin of the antisemitism among certain Christian democrats like Fathers Gayraud and Garnier, otherwise known for their progressive attitude to social

[1] E. Silberner: 'French Socialism and the Jewish Question 1865–1914', *Historia Judaica*, April 1954.

La dernière quille

— Allons, cher baron, encore celle-là... et la partie est à nous.

From the Anti-Dreyfusard *Le Psst!*, February 1898

questions? Such questions indicate the need for elaborate research before the full complexity of racial prejudice can be known. It seems in most cases that antisemitism is a product of social or economic insecurity. Before the Affair there was antisemitism among journalists, artists and intellectuals who were caught up in fierce competition: Drumont's own attitudes follow closely on his initial failure as a journalist. There was antisemitism in that economically unstable and socially fluctuating class known as petit bourgeois, and there was antisemitism among the lower and poorly paid officers in the Army. Less a product of instability than of ideology and class antagonisms was the antisemitism among certain socialists, especially Benoît Malon in the *Revue Socialiste*. And finally, deriving from acute insecurity, political and religious attitudes and local tradition, was the antisemitism of the Catholics and political conservatives whose interests had been seriously undermined by the anticlerical legislation of the Republic.[1] For all these social groupings the Jew provided a natural explanation to their own misfortunes. Only a catalyst was needed to fuse social jealousy or ideological antipathy into active antisemitism. In the 1880s Drumont's book, *La France Juive* (1886), fulfilled such a rôle; in the 1890s it was the Affair. The purpose of Drumont's exposé of French judaism was to denounce the Third Republic as a government controlled by, and a society infested with, scheming self-advancing Jews. Following on a period of republican assertiveness in which Catholics and monarchists had suffered, and coming only a few years after the crash of the great Roman Catholic bank the Union Générale in 1882, it was assured at least of a wide audience among these discontented and resentful elements. Alongside them were others who for reasons already suggested were prey to insecurity and failure. The book rapidly sold over 100,000 copies, many to this gullible public, ready to hold the Jew responsible for their disasters.

Between 1886 and 1894 Drumont in his writings, the Antisemitic League in its activism and a large number of individual antisemites in their journalism and propaganda, played on this public. The Panama scandal of 1892 was grist to their mill, but by 1894 the vehemence of the campaign had abated and the public was less involved. Antisemitism was still a powerful emotion, but its promoters, deprived of active issues, were losing their control. Drumont was even forced to look for buyers for *La Libre Parole*, the paper which had been founded on the crest of the Panama wave. Thus for Drumont and his colleagues

[1] For Catholics and antisemitism see also chapter 3.

the Affair was an economic as well as an emotional necessity, while for the tension between Jews, passive or assertive, on one hand, and antisemites from a variety of social milieux, on the other, it was a catalyst even more explosive than *La France Juive*.

But the importance of the Affair for racial tensions in France was not just the provision of an opportunity for antisemitic outbursts; it did more than this. It crystallised antisemitism and gave it a particular ideological and political character which had been latent but never explicit or organised. In Drumont's following during the late 1880s there was an inchoate mass of political, social and ideological attitudes. What the historian of the Affair has to answer is why antisemitism came to assume conservative, nationalist and right-wing characteristics rather than any other. For example, why did it not become socialist? There had been socialist elements in both Drumont's propaganda and his public. For the socialist the Jew often stood as the arch capitalist, the prototype bourgeois. Why did this vision of the Jew yield so decisively to the nationalist vision of the Jew as an intriguing republican profiteer willing to sell the true interests of France for his own profit? A start towards an explanation of this fact could be made with the following points.

Firstly, one can see from the circulation of Drumont's writings and the reaction to the Panama scandal that antisemitism was most attractive to the opponents and the victims of the Republic. Jews were assimilated into republican politics and the economy to an extent beyond that of Catholics and monarchists, most of whom remained alien to the régime despite the efforts of Pope Leo XIII to effect a reconciliation. Socialists, on the other hand, although political and social outsiders, were as yet far fewer in number, and the antimonarchist, anticlerical persecution had brought them closer to the Republic.

Secondly, antisemitism in France as elsewhere fed largely on fantasy. It was nurtured by such grotesque masquerades as that of Leo Taxil, who, between 1893 and 1897, held a large section of the public in thrall with his stories of Jewish ritual murders, infanticide and sexual perversion. This element of the fantastic depended on a total ignorance of the Jews, and meant that areas without a Jewish population were often susceptible to extreme antisemitism. Such areas were predominantly the country regions of the west; the stronghold of conservative and clerical opinion. In the towns, on the other hand, the reality of labouring Jews, who counterbalanced the Jewish capitalists, tended to dilute any socialist antisemitism that existed. This is not to say that antisemitism was purely a rural phenomenon. Far from it: in the Algerian towns, in Paris, Lyon and Marseille, there was considerable racial tension, due to complex social factors of insecurity and deprivation and the ease with which group passions could be aroused. But urban antisemitism was not a particular political phenomenon, and it was certainly not a consistent by-product of socialism. Rural antisemitism, on the other hand, tended to be more closely linked to existing political and religious attitudes and to produce a more systematic unity of doctrine.

Thirdly, the assertiveness of individual Jews during the Affair was combined in most cases with left-wing republican attitudes. Lazare spoke for the Jewish proletariat, and *L'Univers Israélite* launched an appeal for a combined front against political reaction and clericalism:

> ... already a black crow has sunk its talons into the head of the French cock and has begun systematically to peck out its eyes.[1]

The bird of prey is clericalism, and this vivid intolerant image, though by no means typical of Jewish opinion, was an example of a certain Jewish state of mind which provoked the antagonism of right-wing and clerical elements in society.

Fourthly, although criticism of Jewish capitalists and profiteers continued in socialist pronouncements during the Affair, there were several socialist leaders who from the start saw Drumont's antisemitism as a reactionary force. In the Socialist Manifesto of 19 January 1898 there was the following cynical comment on the Jewish financiers:

> If they could demonstrate with regard to one of their own race that he had been the victim of a judicial mistake and public prejudice they would try to bring about ... the indirect rehabilitation of the whole Jewish Panama group. They would come to this fountain and wash away all the stains of Israel.[2]

But despite such a passage, Jaurès, Lafargue and, less vehemently, Jules Guèsde, all classified antisemitism as a 'capitalist fake', and this attitude was considerably strengthened in those who, like Jaurès, became involved in the Dreyfusard cause.

Lastly, with the triumph of the Dreyfusards, the socialists, led by Jaurès, were no longer such an outsider group,[3] whereas the antisemitic nationalists of the Affair continued, with the interval of the

[1] See Sources, p. 61, no. 1.
[2] See Sources, p. 99, Socialist Manifesto.
[3] See chapter 4.

First World War, to oppose the values of the Third Republic. In the 1930s antisemitism was revived when Léon Blum the Jewish socialist headed the Popular Front. 'Rather Hitler than Blum', the ominous cry of the French Fascists, had a racist as well as a political connotation. Under Vichy this antisemitism was officially endorsed, and it is not by accident that one of the newspapers founded to combat this official racism was called *J'accuse*.

In summary it can be seen that during the Affair antisemitism in France gained a specific right-wing political nuance. It became a facet of that revaluated nationalism which has already been described. Like other passions aroused during the Affair, it was not extinguished by the Rennes verdict, the pardon or the final acquittal. François Mauriac has observed:

> However, with Dreyfus rehabilitated, his accusers routed, his defenders become the masters of power, was there one antisemite less in France or in Europe? Twenty-five years later the eruption of the most atrocious persecution that Israel has ever suffered was evidence of this tragic failure. I doubt whether the Eichmann trial and the horrors which it evokes will be any more effective than the sufferings of one man, in bringing to an end this mysterious hatred, which the mass sacrifice of eight million Jews has failed to appease.[1]

One can challenge Mauriac's argument and disagree with his pessimism, but his comment on the inability of the Affair to stem either French or European antisemitism is justified. It crystallised racial tensions, it did not resolve them.

SOURCES

The Extremes of Antisemitism

1. Morès

The Marquis de Morès was an early national socialist. His motto was 'Life is valuable only through action'. After losing a fortune in wild business adventures he saw the Jews as his persecutors. With Drumont he founded the Antisemitic League and became the activist leader of Jew-baiting thugs. He fought numerous duels, and his writings had the same violence as his

[1] A. Dreyfus: *Cinq ans de ma vie*, 1962 edn. Preface by François Mauriac, p. 20–1.

actions. They are examples of pure fantasy. In this extract he reveals a Jewish plot to sacrifice the Christian children who have mysteriously disappeared. The gullibility of many of his readers should be remembered before it is dismissed as an eccentric curiosity.

D'après les récents arrêts du Grand Kahal secret de la juiverie, dont les faits et gestes n'échappent plus à notre contre-police aryenne, on doit nous faire expier nos sévérités envers Dreyfus par un immense krach financier, par une tuerie franco-allemande et par une série de meurtres rituels. Oui, mères françaises, pour se venger de notre patriotisme les chefs occultes du judaïsme ont décidé qu'en la prochaine année Israël mangerait des azymes saturés de ce sang que le sacrificateur tire des pauvres bébés chrétiens qui disparaissent de temps à autre d'une façon mystérieuse. Seulement cette fois-ci, ce sera une hécatombe et ce sera par centaines que l'on saignera des enfants chrétiens pour la Pâque prochaine. Au point où en sont les choses il faut détruire les Juifs, les chasser jusqu'au dernier de chez nous, ou bien périr par eux.

MARQUIS DE MORÈS, December 1894: quoted in L'Archiviste, *Drumont et Dreyfus*, Stock, 1898, p. 22.

2. Drumont

The journalistic career of Edouard Drumont illustrates as well as any the power of the press during the Affair. His paper La Libre Parole *perpetuated itself by pure polemic: only secondarily was it a news paper. In Drumont himself there was a strange element of socialism, a strong traditionalism and considerable superstition—he was an amateur palmist. In this analysis of Dreyfus there is a perfect blend of all the factors which account for his wide circulation: a pseudo-science based on the Darwinian principle of struggle, a strong determinism ('Jews cannot do otherwise'), a prophetic egoism linked to mock humility and an appeal to religious sensitivity. Dreyfus, he states disarmingly, has not betrayed his country, since he has no country to betray, he is an alien. France is foolish to share her military secrets with such aliens. All that is needed is a qualification for nationality based on three generations of French descent. In resisting this the Jews are preparing their own destruction. Even the Grand Rabbi of France admits that antisemitism holds the future in its hands. But Drumont will not boast of his achievement, he has merely obeyed the voice of a superior will . . .*

L'ÂME DE DREYFUS

En fait, cet homme, si on tient compte de ses origines et de son type a été simplement indélicat; il a fait dans l'armée ce qu'il aurait fait dans une banque ou dans une écurie de courses, il a vendu des tuyaux à la concurrence: il a commis un abus de confiance, mais il n'a pas commis de crime contre la Patrie. Pour trahir sa Patrie il faut en avoir une et le Patrie ne s'acquiert pas avec un acte de naturalisation. La Patrie c'est la terre des aïeux, la terre des pères: les pères de Dreyfus n'étaient pas de notre terre, ils étaient des errands et des nomades partout, et leur fils ne peut se douter de ce que c'est qu'une Patrie. Barrès l'a dit excellemment

> On entend par une nation un groupe d'hommes réunis par des légendes communes, une tradition, des habitudes prises dans un même milieu durant une suite plus ou moins longue d'ancêtres. La naturalisation est une fiction légale que fait participer aux avantages d'une nation, mais ne peut en donner les caractères.

Vous avez été criminels en livrant à des étrangers, à des forains, à ceux qu'à Rome on appelait des *peregrini*, vos secrets les plus sacrés. Vous êtes ridicules en jugeant ceux qui ont abusé de votre imbécile imprévoyance d'après un idéal, des traditions, des conceptions qui ne sont pas les leurs.

Le seul qui me semble avoir un peu de bon sens là-dedans c'est Monsieur de Pontbriand député de la Loire-Inférieure. Au lieu de se livrer à des tirades mélodramatiques il se propose simplement, à ce que nous apprend *l'Autorité*, de demander une chose très juste. Il compte déposer un projet de loi *tendant à rendre obligatoire depuis trois générations au moins, la qualité de Français pour l'accession aux grades ou aux emplois publics*. Les Juifs voués à la Fatalité qui pèse sur eux, s'opposeront éperdument au vote de ce projet. Ils auront tort, et ce n'est pas un conseil d'ennemi que je leur donne en leur conseillant d'accepter cette transaction qui les acclimaterait peu à peu.

Il y a quelque chose de plus puissant que tous ces *Premiers Paris*, toutes les campagnes de journaux stipendiés, toutes ces manœuvres de la Juiverie. Il y a la Force des choses, la résistance invincible des éléments nationaux, l'âme même de la France. En s'obstinant à s'imposer à nous dans les conditions actuelles, à se prétendre impudemment les égaux de ceux dont les pères ont fait la France, les Juifs préparent de leurs propres mains la plus effroyable catastrophe de leur tragique histoire...

Qu'ajouteraient des paroles inutilement violentes à cette constatation d'une si implacable précision.

Quand parut *La France Juive* on dit à Zaddoc-Khan 'C'est un pamphlet'.

— Non, fit-il, c'est une prophétie.

La prophétie s'est réalisée malgré l'apathie des jours actuels, la veulerie de cette nation écœurée plus encore qu'indignée de toutes ces hontes, les colères grondent partout à l'heure présente. Si demain les événements jetaient leur drame sur toutes ces passions incandescentes, si la France était prise de cette fièvre patriotique qui la saisit aux époques de crise, un gouffre s'ouvrirait en plein Paris comme il s'en ouvrit un en plein Forum, au moment de la guerre des Samnites. Il engloutirait la race maudite sans que nul Curtius offrît sa vie pour apaiser le courroux des dieux.

Et cependant... *La France Juive* date de 1886! Il y a huit ans de cela et c'est bien peu pour la marche d'une idée. Quel courant d'opinions toutes faites il fallait remonter à cette époque et quels reins solides il fallait avoir alors pour soutenir presque seul un combat, dont des collaborateurs vaillants et jeunes allègent le poids aujourd'hui!

Seigneur, je ne m'enorgueillis pas de cet effort. J'ai toujours été le plus faible, le plus sentimental, le plus facile à décourager de tous les hommes, et l'opiniâtre courage que j'ai montré pour éclairer mon pays, presque malgré lui c'est vous qui me l'avez donné... *Ecce Deus adjuvat me, et Dominus est susceptor animae meae: averte mala enimicis meis, et in veritate tua disperde illos, protector meus, Domine.*

... Ceci je tiens à le dire à tous ceux qui m'envoyent des félicitations et des encouragements, à ceux qui étaient prévenus contre moi et qui reconnaissent maintenant que j'avais raison et plus particulièrement encore à nos jeunes amis des comités antisémitiques, qui s'organisent un peu partout à Paris, à Lyon, à Dijon, à Montpellier.

Mes livres auront rendu un immense service à notre chère France, en lui révélant le péril Juif, en l'empêchant d'être livrée pieds et poings liés à l'ennemi, au moment d'une guerre, par les Dreyfus et les Reinach, embusqués dans tous les services importants. Ces livres je suis heureux de les avoir écrits, mais je ne mérite pas qu'on me loue à ce sujet, car je ne pouvais pas ne pas les écrire. Une volonté supérieure me disait 'Parle!' J'ai parlé.

EDOUARD DRUMONT: *La Libre Parole*, 26 December 1894.

Two Polemics: Jew and Catholic

1. 'L'Univers Israélite'
This weekly paper, self styled 'Preserver of the principles of Judaism', had a small circulation and is rarely quoted in works on the Affair. But it provided for the antisemites a perfect example of the Jewish policy of solidarity which they so vehemently decried. Seen objectively, it is as aggressively anticlerical as La Croix is antisemite (see following extract). The opening of this article is a stark, direct accusation: clericalism is responsible for the Affair. It continues by describing the methods of the Jesuits, whom it accuses of using every crisis against the Republic. But the Jews and republicans are to blame for not unmasking the antisemite, for not understanding the clerical subversion. Isn't Drumont himself the puppet of the Jesuits? Only the Protestants have seen clearly. Liberty is threatened, forces of reaction are growing. Organisation and defensive war is needed: all thinking men are locked in the same struggle with the clerical enemy. Finally it calls for an alliance of Jews, Protestants and Freemasons to fight for liberty and light.

LES FAUTES PASSÉES ET LE DEVOIR PRÉSENT

... Il est évident que l'Affaire Dreyfus est une effroyable machine que le cléricalisme a montée contre les juifs et contre la République, c'est-à-dire contre la Liberté et contre la pensée.

... Certes la République avec sa liberté égale pour tous et sa neutralité en matière confessionnelle était de nature à porter le mécontentement des cléricaux au paroxysme de la colère. Ah! ils étaient bien malheureux! Ils bouillaient de fureur, et ils ne pouvaient l'exhaler, cette fureur, car la masse du suffrage universel était contre eux: leurs cris auraient trahi leurs désirs et achevé de ruiner leur ambition.

Alors ils ont usé du moyen cher aux jésuites. Ils ont travaillé en dessous, ils ont organisé un immense complot souterrain, ils ont fait naître les scandales les plus nauséeux, ils en ont couvert la France afin de discréditer le régime républicain; ils ont brassé le boulangisme, ils ont brassé le Panama, ils ont brassé l'affaire Dreyfus. Ils se sont alliés à la lie de la populace; toutes les décompositions morales ont communié; les odeurs de la sacristie mêlaient leur parfum rance aux senteurs des égouts.

Si le boulangisme et le Panama ont été comme les béliers d'airain au moyen desquels ils ont fait brèche dans les remparts de la République, l'affaire Dreyfus a été leur cheval de Troie, car ils sont dans la place. Et grâce à qui? Grâce à l'aveuglement du parti républicain et grâce à l'inertie des juifs. Oui, les Israélites sont coupables de n'avoir pas dès le début essayé d'enrayer la campagne qui se dessinait contre eux. Ils sont demeurés le sourire aux lèvres et haussant dédaigneusement les épaules. Ils parlaient d'un feu de paille et croyaient impossible un réveil des vieux préjugés.

... Quant au parti républicain il a complètement manqué de clairvoyance. Il s'est soucié de la campagne antisémite comme d'une feuille morte. Il n'a pas su démasquer le froc clérical sous la défroque antijuive. Cependant les intentions étaient faciles à percer: n'attaquait-on pas avec la même virulence et pêle-mêle juifs, protestants et francs-maçons? *La Libre Parole* ne se posait-elle pas en champion du catholicisme et ne couvrait-elle pas chaque jour, dans chaque ligne de chacune de ses colonnes, le régime actuel d'opprobre et d'ignominie? N'était-il pas évident pour quiconque réfléchissait que Drumont était le pantin dont les jésuites tenaient et tiraient les ficelles?

... Seuls entre tous, les protestants ont vu clair dans les manœuvres ennemies et ont dénoncé dans leurs journaux et leurs revues la résurrection cléricale. Hommage leur soit rendu pour leur perspicacité et aussi surtout pour la vaillance dont ils ont fait preuve. Un parti et une religion qui comptent des hommes comme MM. Scheurer-Kestner, Monod, Trarieux, et tant d'autres sont un parti et une religion forte et à qui la victoire est assurée sur la lâcheté et l'obscurantisme. Juifs mes frères, prenons modèle sur les protestants français.

En ce moment nous sommes en pleine réaction, cela est perçant d'évidence. Or les élections générales approchent: si le public n'est pas détrompé, la liberté court les plus graves dangers. Il ne s'agit donc pas de demeurer les bras ballants ni de nous répandre en stériles jérémiades. Assez et trop longtemps nous nous sommes montrés d'une légèreté criminelle et nous avons suivi une politique d'autruche. Groupons-nous, organisons-nous et concentrons-nous en vue de refouler l'adversaire; ceignons nos reins et jetons-nous dans la mêlée. Que chacun de nous fasse la plus active des propagandes en faveur de la justice et de la vérité. Toute nouvelle défaillance hâterait notre défaite et celle des hautes idées qui font le prix de la vie et l'honneur de l'humanité. Du reste, et heureusement, nous ne sommes pas seuls à combattre le bon combat; tout ce qui *pense* marche avec nous.

A nous donc juifs, protestants, francs-maçons et quiconque veut la lumière et la liberté, de nous serrer les coudes et de lutter pour que la

France, comme dit une de nos prières, conserve son rang glorieux parmi les nations, car déjà un sombre corbeau a planté ses griffes sur le crâne du coq gaulois et se met en devoir de lui becqueter les yeux.

LOUIS LÉVY: *L'Univers Israélite*, 21 January 1898.

2. 'La Croix'

The title of this editorial, 'Feu Ouvert', is significant. Father Vincent de Paul Bailly had taken a trip to the Holy Land and did not return to his paper until 26 January 1898. Before this date La Croix *had taken a clear stand on the culpability of Dreyfus and had made short attacks on the so-called Jewish Syndicate. But it was only after Zola's* J'accuse *and the return of* Le moine *to the editor's seat that the paper launched this full offensive against its enemies. The Assumptionists, of which* La Croix *was the main organ, were always politically conscious and appointed themselves as the defenders of the religious orders (congrégations) in France. Bailly's own particular vehemence led them into a position of aggression and* La Croix *became one of the most outspoken anti-Dreyfusard, antisemitic papers. In this article Bailly sets the Catholic world against all those forces which* L'Univers Israélite *had invoked. The Jews, he says, believed they could crush the church and its orders: they controlled the press, the civil service and much of the electorate. Zola's indecency and sacrilege have been acclaimed by the people. But the tide is turning. In Algeria the threat of the Jews is understood. In the chamber a ridiculous brawl (see Sources, p. 97, no. 2) showed the danger of the Jews whose money has infiltrated into politics. Politicians are now only too keen to emancipate themselves from this influence, and the people have rejected the filthy Zola. They have turned to Catholic France. The army has been forced to open fire: war is on.*

FEU OUVERT

On va lire l'étonnant procès qui éclate aujourd'hui comme un due entre l'armée et le syndicat juif appuyé 'par la triplice et l'inévitable anglo-saxon'.

Sans doute c'est la patrie en danger qui s'insurge contre l'ennemi déjà répandu sur le territoire; mais il faut être aveugle pour ne pas reconnaître le prodigieux changement qui amène aujourd'hui une lutte, déclarée impossible en cette fin de siècle entre la France catholique et la France juive, protestante et libre-penseuse.

Oh! certainement les vainqueurs des Loges ne croyaient pas que des questions catholiques pussent encore passioner la France avachie.

Cependant les Loges juives avaient déjà éprouvé en ces derniers temps, une stupéfaction de la résistance imprévue des Congrégations.

Les juifs, en imaginant les lois fiscales, croyaient qu'ils écrasaient des insectes impuissants, et le Christ vit encore, après qu'ils l'ont scellé sous la grosse pierre.

Néanmoins la lutte dans la presse sur la place publique, contre la libre-pensée était bien impossible.

Le très immonde Zola avait outragé notre Sauveur sous les formes les plus horribles, donnant son Nom divin à d'immondes personnages: il avait écrit *Lourdes* contre la Vierge Immaculée, *Rome* contre l'Église, et l'opinion publique l'avait acclamé, payant au poids de l'or jusqu'aux expressions qu'on n'avait jamais imprimées qu'au dictionnaire selon l'ordre alphabétique.

Les juifs avaient admiré ce géant de l'opinion qui piétinait le Christ, la Vierge et l'Église en soulevant des applaudissements et ils avaient acheté à grands prix sa plume et son fumier.

Que pouvions-nous contre toute la presse? tout le fonctionnarisme? toute la finance? et le suffrage?

Au retour de Terre Sainte où l'on avait médité de notre faiblesse au pied de la croix, sur le Calvaire délaissé et outragé, nous fûmes étonnés de trouver à Marseille un magasin juif pillé; des dépêches nous annonçaient que les Algériens, peu dévots écrivaient sur leurs devantures: *Maison catholique: Ici, il y a des chrétiens et pas de juifs* etc.

Le soir même, à propos de la question juive et alors que Jaurès disait que l'état-major n'était qu'une jésuitière, les députés se livraient à un pugilat qui n'avait rien des jeux olympiques. Un gavroche (il est vrai qu'il n'est plus académicien que M. Zola) s'écriait avec franchise: 'Ils se sont... une "peignée".'

Le monde financier juif qui tient tous les personnages du théâtre politique avec des ficelles d'or, voyait ses pantins se tordre, on ne parlait plus que de s'émanciper.

Juifs et protestants sont enfin réputés dangereux par le peuple: celui-ci n'écoute plus les politiques en vogue, pas même Zola le glorieux ordurier; les événements tournent si singulièrement, que ces infidèles et hérétiques ont dû attaquer l'armée et que celle-ci, en se défendant des soufflets les plus retentissants, entame ce soir le procès contre les ennemis reconnus du Christ et de l'Église. Elle s'appuie sur la France catholique.

C'est donc la libre-pensée couronnée hier et avocate des juifs, des protestants et de tous les ennemis de la France, qui est sur la sellette de Zola et l'armée est obligée, malgré elle, d'ouvrir le feu.

L'incendie ne va pas s'éteindre.

'LE MOINE' (Père V. de P. Bailly): *La Croix*, 8 February 1898.

Antisemitism: Two Analyses

1. Herzl

Theodore Herzl, the Zionist leader, was an acute, if partisan, observer of the Affair. In this report to a German newspaper, Die Welt, *on 24 December 1897, he diagnosed a deep-seated racialism in the French people. He begins by describing the apparent finality of the judgment of 1894. Dreyfus is condemned by public passions to stay in his island imprisonment. But the notion that he might be innocent is spreading, helped by new revelations. Revision, however, is barred. For political reasons Dreyfus must not be innocent: to admit that he is would be to risk an explosion of public fury. Dreyfus must suffer. But for whom? There have been other traitors without such a storm. Why such public fury now? Because he is a Jew. Even the officers of the court-martial feared this public prejudice. It is not as if Dreyfus is connected with the big Jewish financiers, but he is hated just for being a Jew. France is antisemitic, from the conservatives to the extreme left. Will Dreyfus be the last victim? The whole crisis shows the weakness of the government, which is made up of Opportunists. (See chapter 4.) In order to keep themselves in power they are prepared to sacrifice the Jews. Passions alone will decide the issue. (For de Mun's speech see p. 95, and for the charge that Opportunists and Jews are in alliance see also the Socialist Manifesto, p. 99.)*

LA SITUATION EN FRANCE

Quelques hommes fidèles et courageux ont essayé de soulever la lourde pierre qui recouvre sa tombe. Mais une meute déchaînée se jeta sur les libérateurs et les écarta. La pierre tombale a repris ainsi sa place antérieure et l'être vivant continue à rester enseveli. Tel est l'aspect actuel de l'Affaire Dreyfus de triste renom. Le peuple de France si généreux, si avide de justice, le peuple des Droits de l'Homme qui révise tous les procès et n'admet jamais un jugement irrévocable, se récuse de remettre en doute la culpabilité du capitaine juif.

Les manifestations bruyantes de la rue, les déclamations patriotiques à la Chambre, les injures des journaux tous ensemble ne poursuivent qu'un seul but: garder ce Juif dans l'Ile du Diable. Ils le tuent encore alors qu'il est déjà enseveli. Et il faut penser à ce proverbe 'Quand on est mort c'est pour longtemps'. D'autant plus si c'est le sort d'un vivant car il est bien retranché des vivants pour longtemps.

Cependant dans l'esprit et dans le cerveau de quelques hommes pas trop méchants et non seulement des Israélites a germé l'idée que le pauvre homme dans son île équatoriale, à qui ses galons de capitaine furent arrachés par leur faute, que ce pauvre juif serait innocent. Ni les bruits de la rue, ni les articles incendiaires de certains journaux ne peuvent plus expulser cette idée de celui qui la fait sienne et qui porte le deuil de cet être vivant. On peut le dire que la conduite contradictoire et douleuse du gouvernement français, dictée en toute évidence par son désir de conservation, n'a nullement réussi à dissiper le doute. Les faits nouveaux, actuellement connus, auraient paru dans tout autre procès suffisamment importants pour justifier une révision. Même si nous pouvions admettre à la rigueur qu'un deuxième procès puisse à nouveau se terminer par une condamnation, cela constituerait au moins une prise en considération de l'opinion publique, troublée dans son sentiment de justice.

Mais les faits sont ainsi. On se refuse à refaire le procès, parce que le capitaine Dreyfus ne doit pas être innocent. Le peuple pourrait croire, dit-on, qu'il a été trompé et victime d'une comédie judiciaire, montée de toutes pièces par des financiers juifs en vue de la libération d'un des leurs. On pourrait craindre alors une explosion violente de la colère populaire.

Telles semblent avoir été les raisons d'Etat qui tendent à justifier le rejet des demandes de révision. Il se peut que le cabinet ne pouvait agir autrement dans cette dangereuse affaire car gouverner n'est souvent que choisir entre deux injustices. On peut même supposer que tel ou tel Israélite français préférerait que cette tragédie se termine par la mort d'un seul.

... La souffrance amère de cet homme a soulevé une question d'une importance autrement considérable: Pour qui paie-t-il? Pour qui?

... Nous pensons ... à ces groupes et personnes, à qui le prisonnier doit ses souffrances. Il en existe, sans aucun doute. Admettons un court instant que Dreyfus aurait commis réellement ce crime. D'autres avant lui ont été condamnés et encore dernièrement quelques cas semblables ont été découverts au sein de l'armée française. Mais jamais de telles clameurs ont accompagné les traîtres dans leur déshonneur. Toute la fureur déchaînée a été réservée à Dreyfus. La populace l'aurait, si cela avait été possible, roulé dans du goudron, écartelé, commis je ne sais quelle torture. Pourquoi donc? Ce n'étaient plus des cris de vengeance contre une trahison militaire, qui, d'habitude, passionne peu les foules en temps de paix. Cette explosion de colère était d'une nature toute différente, semblable aux excès d'une bande d'émeutiers et de gens en révolte. Ils faisaient bien peu de cas de l'accusation. Ils ne hurlaient pas 'A bas Dreyfus' mais 'A bas les Juifs'. C'était ainsi dès le début et cela continuait. C'est en effet sur la base d'un bordereau, d'une authenticité combien suspecte que le capitaine Dreyfus fut traîné devant un tribunal, composé de sept juges militaires dont l'honneur était irréprochable.

Mais ces juges-officiers subissaient des pressions intolérables et c'est justement à cause de l'huis clos que la pression de l'opinion publique fut aussi monstreuse. Ces sept braves, qui ne tremblent sans doute jamais pour leur vie, ont dû tout de même trembler pour leur honneur. Car dehors dans la rue, la calomnie épiait ses victimes. Ne racontait-on pas, dès le début, l'ignoble histoire de l'argent juif qui devait délivrer le traître?

Pauvre Juif chargé de la malédiction de l'argent, de l'argent des autres: il n'avait rien à faire avec eux, ni eux avec lui, mais immédiatement on les disait alliés.

Puisqu'on ne pouvait saisir ceux qu'on haïssait on haïssait celui dont on pouvait se saisir. L'Affaire Dreyfus a révélé ainsi, en France, une telle accumulation de haine contre les Juifs, qu'on ne pouvait a priori soupçonner qui en porte la responsabilité. Nullement ce courageux capitaine d'artillerie, originaire d'Alsace, prêt à donner sa vie pour la France sur les champs de bataille. Un député a osé demander à la Chambre de ce pays républicain, qu'aucun Israélite ne soit désormais admis au service de l'Etat. Une proposition similaire, mais un peu moins précise, avait été déposée il y a quelques années à l'occasion de l'affaire du Canal de Panama, et rejetée par 160 voix. Si cette proposition venait à être soumise aujourd'hui combien voteraient pour elle?

La France d'aujourd'hui est antisémite, cela ne fait pas de doute. *Le Figaro*, l'un des journaux les plus riches et les plus influents qui avait pendant un certain temps pris la défense de Dreyfus, fut contraint par l'opinion publique à capituler. Le rédacteur en chef a dû démissionner pour ne pas mettre en danger l'existence même du journal. Et pourtant un journaliste de l'importance d'un rédacteur en chef du *Figaro* est bien plus libre et plus indépendant qu'un député, dont la popularité est bien instable. Les scandales parlementaires de ces dernières années avaient considérablement diminué leur prestige. Oseraient-ils, même s'ils le pensaient autrement, s'opposer aux passions de la populace? Les élections approchent et il est facile de prévoir que l'antisémitisme en sera le cheval de bataille.

Des conservateurs à l'extrême-gauche on n'entend qu'un seul cri 'contre les Juifs'. C'est une ambiance des temps d'émeute et ceux que cette affaire intéresse en premier lieu sont sourds et aveugles : ils pensent toujours que cela passera. Certes, tout se passe, mais de quelle manière?

Croit-on vraiment que les mangeurs de Juifs qui ont éprouvé leur force sur le malheureux Dreyfus se contenteront d'une seule victime? Ils ont pris le goût du sang et ils en demanderont encore avec d'autant plus d'assurance et d'avidité qu'ils ont pris conscience de leur puissance irrésistible.

Toute cette affaire a rendu manifeste la faiblesse et la regrettable indécision de l'autorité gouvernementale de la France. Lorsque la digue cède, les eaux tumultueuses se préparent à jaillir. Les intérêts des conservateurs ne coïncident pas d'habitude avec ceux du gouvernement, même s'ils font partie de la majorité. Le discours follement applaudi du Comte de Mun prouve que même les conservateurs sont contre les Juifs. Il n'y a que chez les opportunistes que les Juifs trouvent un soutien combien faible, parce que, intimidés ils n'osent prendre la parole.

On entend dire que l'opportunisme a fait faillite à cause des Juifs. Il semble plus juste de dire que les Juifs vont à la catastrophe à cause de l'opportunisme. Les radicaux et les partis réactionnaires sont contre eux et les partis du centre ne peuvent se maintenir qu'en sacrifiant les Juifs. Amis, comme on le voit, la situation est sérieuse en France. Il ne s'agit plus du tout du pauvre capitaine dégradé, à qui ses ennemis les plus acharnés ne reprochent plus d'avoir tiré un avantage matériel de son crime hypothétique ... Alors il ne sera plus question de faute ou d'innocence, ni de justice.

C'est la passion seule qui tranchera le débat.

T. HERZL : *L'Affaire Dreyfus*, Fédération sioniste de France, s.d.

2. Meyer

Although he was also of Jewish origin, Arthur Meyer became an anti-Dreyfusard and a regular diner at the salon of Mme de Loynes, where the

Ligue de la Patrie Française was organised. The reason for his attitude in the Affair was his ideal of order and authority, of which the army was the guardian. He was scornful of the Republic and accused it of creating social divisions and chaos by its anticlericalism. His writings are clear and forceful, a colourful mixture of perception and reactionary bias. In this passage he sees antisemitism, not like Herzl as a psychological obsession, but as a defence against anticlericalism. When anticlericalism is dead, antisemitism will die also. The Republic, he begins, is really responsible, since Jules Ferry in his anticlerical legislation relied on Jews, Freethinkers and Freemasons. The Republic has idolised money. The remedy is to restore religion and a real central authority. Idols must be broken, and true élites re-established. The balance in France must be restored not by the exclusion of Jews but by reducing them to their proper place, relative to their merit and number.

J'ai dit que l'antisémitisme était une fleur vénéneuse née sur le fumier républicain. Je vais expliquer ma pensée. C'est en effet la république qui, en portant la puissance juive à son maximum pour l'associer plus utilement à sa politique d'agression sauvage, a soulevé la passion de la revanche chez les moins violents d'entre les catholiques, a provoqué toutes les résistances, a fortifié et justifié l'antisémitisme aux yeux de beaucoup de Français. L'antisémitisme est donc bien l'œuvre des républicains. Pour attaquer les catholiques, pour déchristianiser la France, Jules Ferry devait s'appuyer naturellement sur trois forces hostiles aux catholiques, les juifs, les libres-penseurs et surtout les francs-maçons; et les juifs, les libres-penseurs et les francs-maçons ont domestiqué la république.

... La république a gouverné pour les juifs contre les catholiques, et l'antisémitisme est né et s'est développé, comme une pieuse protestation. La république s'est approprié le fameux mot: 'Ni Dieu, ni maître', et elle s'est empressée de déifier l'argent, notre unique souverain aujourd'hui; elle a décapité toutes les aristocraties et elle s'est mise au service de la féodalité financière; elle a ouvert toutes grandes les portes des forteresses administratives, diplomatiques, militaires à tous ceux qui voulaient la servir dans son œuvre révolutionnaire. Voilà la coupable, voilà le mal. L'indiquer c'est faire pressentir le remède. Il faut rétablir Dieu, il faut restaurer le Maître. Il faut faire une guerre impitoyable à l'argent, s'il veut n'être qu'un but avilissant et non un moyen fécond. Il faut briser le Veau d'or. Moïse, qui fut un bon juif, nous en a donné l'exemple, et sans chercher notre modèle aussi loin, nous pouvons imiter simplement l'ancien président des Etats-Unis, qui mène contre les trusts, qui sont rarement juifs, une campagne ardente. En face de l'aristocratie de l'or, reconstituons la hiérarchie du talent, rendons à toutes les élites, de la naissance comme de l'intelligence, la place qu'elles méritent et que l'or a voulu leur enlever, pour agir sur les appétits déchaînés.

Je demande à M. Drumont la permission de lui rappeler une de ses paroles les plus heureuses. Il a dit: 'La France aux Français.' Ne peut-on ajouter: 'A tous les Français' sans distinction d'origine, de confession ou d'opinion, pourvu qu'ils soient enfants de France bien enracinés? L'Angleterre a compté d'illustres serviteurs parmi les juifs; deux entre autres, Disraeli et Léopold de Rothschild, sont entrés à la Chambre des lords pour les grands services qu'ils avaient rendus à leur patrie. En honorant leur patriotisme, elle les avait offerts en exemple aux autres juifs. L'exemple est bon. Remettons les juifs dans le rang ni au-dessus ni au-dessous des autres Français, au niveau et à la mesure de leur mérite et de leur nombre.

A. MEYER: *Ce que mes yeux ont vu*, Plon, 1911, pp. 128–32.

III
Religious Tensions

'France, you are heading back to the church; you are returning to the past, to the intolerant and theocratic past which your most eminent sons have fought with their skill and their blood.'

This was Zola in his open *Lettre à la France* on 6 January 1898.[1] In reply *La Croix*, the journal of the Assumptionists, portrayed Zola lifting the round lid of a lavatory seat, holding it against his ear and speaking into the opening as into a telephone: 'Hullo, Hullo, put me through to France will you?' The two images, the reactionary Catholic and the indecent anticlerical, were two of the most widespread stereotypes of the Affair. Equally intolerant in conception and application, they blinded contemporaries to the greater complexity of the religious problem. It appeared that anticlericals and Catholics stood in closed ranks with no internal dissension.

The conflict dates from the eighteenth century and the Revolution; it was developed by the alliance of Church and Second Empire against liberalism and republicanism in the 1850s, and it reached breaking point in the 1870s and 1880s when the educational and political system was overhauled to eliminate clerical influence. In the decade before Dreyfus, Pope Leo XIII had encouraged French Catholics to rally to the Republic, but the Ralliement, despite the collaboration of conservative republicans under Méline and republican Catholics under Jacques Piou, had not succeeded in appeasing the ingrained hostility of the broad mass of Catholics to a régime which had openly discriminated against them. The Dreyfus Affair in simple terms ranged inveterate anticlericals against equally vehement Catholics; a view which is perhaps the most accessible interpretation of the Affair.

To explain the intensity of this antagonism would be to write the history of Catholic thought and policy in the nineteenth century, as well as an analysis of secularism. It was more than a conflict of faith and reason. The Catholic faith was harnessed to a collection of political

[1] See Sources, p. 81, no. 1, Zola.

and social attitudes which together formed a unitary doctrine. Secular reason in a similar way had its own unitary view of life. The secularisation of education in the late 1870s was intended to promote a rationalist philosophy in the schools and universities, and positivism, the native French creed of the nineteenth century, had a dogmatism of its own; all questions could in the end be confronted and answered by scientific application. Thus Catholicism, with its denunciation of left-wing politics and its hierarchical social doctrines, appeared to trespass into non-religious fields, while secularism, with its philosophy of man and life, appeared to challenge religious belief. The all-pervading claims of both systems made constant tension inevitable. There were, of course, many who cut across this division: liberal Catholics, like Lacordaire and Montalembert under the Second Empire, who attempted to reconcile Catholicism with the revolutionary tradition of France; liberal republicans, like Jules Simon, who in the 1870s wanted to reduce clerical privilege but not to attack belief; and the policies of Popes and French governments fluctuated from intolerance to compromise. Leo XIII, who followed the intransigent Pius IX in 1878, was flexible in his politics and innovatory in his social policies: the government of Méline from 1896 to 1898 firmly rejected the anticlericalism of the 1880s. But when the Dreyfus Affair burst on France with the trial of Esterhazy and Zola's *J'accuse* in January 1898 its particular characteristics conditioned most anticlericals to become pro-Dreyfus and most Catholics to be against him. Emotionally and ideologically the two systems were tempered to follow through their divisions into the Affair and to make of the crisis a battleground for their respective values. From the start of the Affair anticlericals found it easy to see the hand of reaction behind the injustice which the revisionists had discovered, and the Catholics found it easy to see in this revisionist campaign a renewed attack on their interests and beliefs. The acute self-consciousness of both sides, and the deeply rooted conviction of inevitable antipathy made the controversy over one man's conviction into a passionate conflict between Catholic and Secular France.

But if it is true that this basic division obtained during the Affair, there are certain details which need to be asserted to make the simple picture a more complex and accurate one.

In the first place, one of the most enduring myths of the Affair needs to be finally repudiated. Stemming mainly from Reinach and perpetuated in a number of secondhand accounts, it states that the Jesuits, organised by a particular priest Père du Lac, were the insidious sponsors of the Affair. This is almost entirely false, but it has persisted even though the Enquiry which dealt with the revision of the verdict of Rennes completely exonerated the Jesuit Father. The image of a so-called saintly man directing affairs from the confessional was an alluring one and played for polemical Dreyfusards the same rôle that the myth of the Jewish syndicate played for the antisemites. The basis of the accusation against the Jesuits was the success of the Jesuit college in the Rue des Postes in preparing pupils for the higher echelons of the army. It was said that the Postards, old boys of the college, made an antisemitic clique in the General Staff while their former teacher and confessor Père du Lac was the evil genius behind them. Louis Capéran's studies have convincingly reduced this accusation to mere supposition and anti-Jesuit prejudice.[1] Du Lac may have been the friend and the confessor of certain anti-Dreyfusards, including General Boisdeffre, but there is no evidence that he influenced the course of the Affair. If the Jesuit machinations were so organised one may ask how Picquart, a Postard, slipped through the net? Even more unfounded was the accusation of Georges Sorel against the Vatican. If anything, Leo XIII believed in the innocence of Dreyfus.

The group of Catholics who did become the virulent mouthpiece of anti-Dreyfusism was the religious order of the Assumptionists through their journalist, Father Vincent de Paul Bailly. In his paper *La Croix*, Bailly indulged in antisemitism and a fervent campaign against Protestants and Freethinkers.[2] It was ironic that Leo XIII had chosen the Assumptionists as his agents in the Ralliement, and this double game played by the Order brings them little credit. They were suppressed in 1900 by Waldeck-Rousseau's government for the extremism of their electoral campaigns in 1898: their influence had been widely diffused through their chain of newspapers: with Drumont's *Libre Parole* they had sown antisemitism and anti-Dreyfusism throughout rural Catholicism.

Undoubtedly this Catholic antisemitism was no Dreyfusard fiction. A large percentage of parish priests were of peasant origin with ingrained social prejudices against the Jews. The publisher P. V. Stock gives an example of peasant antisemitism:

> In Lorraine—at that time anyway—there were no Jews in the villages. If one came it was only occasionally to buy or sell something. However, they were sometimes sent for in order to kill a sheep or a calf, a cow or a

[1] L. Capéran: *L'Anticléricalisme et l'Affaire Dreyfus*, 1948, pp. 264–72.
[2] See Sources, p. 63, no. 2, *La Croix*.

Populo. — Est-ce une Croix ou un Sabre ?...

From the Dreyfusard *Le Sifflet*, 10 March 1898

bull, since the peasants themselves would kill only their pigs and farmyard animals; and when these Jewish butchers had completed their job and left the village the small boys—of whom I was one—followed, throwing stones at them.[1]

In such communities the Jew was an outsider to be laughed at, and, if the occasion demanded, despised and hated.

But one manifestation of Catholic antisemitism was grossly exaggerated by Dreyfusards. After the suicide of Colonel Henry, a fund was opened on 13 December 1898 by *La Libre Parole* to support his 'widow and orphan against the Jew Reinach'. Subscribers were numerous, and among them were several Catholic priests who accompanied their subscriptions with evocations of 'la Patrie' or antisemitic insults. One priest named Cros, for example, contributed five francs 'for a bedside rug made of the skins of Jews in order to tread on them every morning and evening'. A sociological division of the subscribers was compiled by a Dreyfusard Pierre Quillard,[2] and in the section marked 'Clergy' there were some three hundred names. For anticlericals this was sufficient evidence that the whole Catholic establishment was anti-Dreyfusard and antisemitic. In fact, three hundred clergy was a mere fraction of the 50,000 priests in France. Moreover, there was little direct interference in the Affair by the Catholic hierarchy.

Perhaps the feature of the Affair most ignored by contemporaries was the existence of a dedicated group of Catholic Dreyfusards. For obvious reasons their strength and their ideas were concealed by anticlericals and Catholic anti-Dreyfusards alike. Continuing the liberal-Catholic tradition of Lacordaire, Montalembert and Piou, they had few resources and no newspaper, but wrote pamphlets and books, and since some were priests, the pulpit and pastoral visitation was open to them. But they reached a minimal percentage of public opinion. Léon Chaine, one of their number, wrote that it was almost impossible for a Catholic to be a Dreyfusard, 'It was like the eighth deadly sin, if it was not erected into a monstrous heresy'.[3] This is something of an embittered generalisation, but another Catholic Dreyfusard, Abbé Brugerette, endorsed it, and the impression given by his writings is one of heavy official disapproval for his pro-Dreyfus sympathies. The

[1] P. V. Stock: *Mémorandum d'un Editeur. L'Affaire Dreyfus anecdotique*, 1938, p. 14.
[2] See Sources, p. 82, no. 2, Quillard.
[3] Abbé H. de Saint-Poli (Abbé J. Brugerette): *L'Affaire Dreyfus et la mentalité catholique en France*, 1904, p. 11.

most influential of the group was Paul Viollet, who turned from the anticlerical Ligue des Droits de l'Homme to found the Comité Catholique pour la défense du Droit. He and the abbés Pichot, Frémont and Brugerette were the most eloquent exponents of their cause: Abbé Pichot wrote one particularly cogent open letter arguing that antisemitism was fundamentally unchristian.[1]

Like communists who anticipate the party line, Viollet, Pichot and their colleagues were at first rejected and later rehabilitated by Catholicism. Of great significance for the development of Christian Democracy in twentieth-century France, they were only a handful during the Affair. Viollet's Catholic Committee had no more than two hundred members. But the existence of even this small grouping gave the lie to the anticlerical generalisation that Catholics were inevitably enemies of progressive France.

The triumph of the anticlericals came with the government of Combes in 1902. During the Affair anticlericalism had been the main characteristic of *La Dépêche de Toulouse*; it had permeated the writings of Zola, Clemenceau and Jaurès; it was important to the polemic of the *Univers Israélite* and it underlay the Dreyfusism of Yves Guyot in *Le Siècle* and Arthur Ranc in *Le Radical*. But in Emile Combes, once an equally vehement Catholic novice, it reached its zenith, and the illiberality of his legislation which led logically to the separation of church and state in 1905 antagonised even the former anticlerical Clemenceau. But the separation, although at the time fiercely contested by the church, allowed a gradual rapprochement of Catholicism and republicanism on the recognition that each had its independent interests and sphere of influence. Although enmity died hard and the religious conflicts of the Affair continued to influence large sections of opinion, the growth of a Catholic republican spirit could be no longer ignored in the France of the 1930s and 1940s. Under Vichy the hierarchy of the church was not inclined to oppose Pétain, but an important number of confessing Catholics took part in the Resistance, and in postwar France the Christian Democrat party (MRP: Mouvement Républicain Populaire) has been integral to the politics of the Fourth and Fifth Republics.

In retrospect therefore, although not at the time, the Affair and its Combist sequel appears to be the last explosion of religious tensions in modern France. At least in one respect the violent passions of the Affair brought to some extent their own appeasement. But over certain

[1] Abbé Pichot: *La conscience Chrétienne et l'Affaire Dreyfus*, 1899.

problems of education and in tradition-conscious communities the tension continues. Secular and Catholic France still have differences to resolve.

SOURCES

Catholic Anti-Dreyfusism

1. Dreyfus as the Devil

For many ordinary Catholics anti-Dreyfusism was a natural reaction. Dreyfus had betrayed France. It was not surprising that Catholic sailors should cross themselves when passing the scene of his imprisonment.

En 1898 me rendant en France mon bateau passa en vue de l'Ile du Diable où Dreyfus était interné. Ayant remarqué que les matelots, bretons fervents catholiques (originaires de St Nazaire, leur port d'attache) se signaient à plusieurs reprises, je demandai au commandant si c'était pour conjurer les maléfices du diable dont cette île portait le nom. 'Pas du tout,' me répondait-il, 'c'est seulement depuis que Dreyfus y est.' Il était donc, à leurs yeux, pire que le diable.

LE COMTE DE ST AULAIRE: *Confession d'un vieux diplomate*, Flammarion, 1953, p. 47.

2. Pastoral guidance: Mgr Mathieu

Although there was little overt interference by the Catholic hierarchy during the Affair, there were some bishops, such as Mgr Mathieu of Toulouse, who made their opinion perfectly clear to their clergy and congregations. In this Lenten letter Mgr Mathieu demonstrates that unquestioning acceptance of authority and military judgments which was the mark of most anti-Dreyfusards. He deprecates the campaign against the army and the accusations against Esterhazy: although he is officially a minister of peace he knows where his allegiance lies. (The frontier referred to is the Franco-German one, continually in dispute since the seizure of Alsace Lorraine by Bismarck in 1871.)

Vous êtes encore tout émus, n'est-il pas vrai?, de la campagne si funeste qui vient d'être menée contre nos chefs militaires, de cette insurrection contre la justice, de cette tentative de réhabilitation d'un traître et de ces efforts acharnés et malhonnêtes pour charger un innocent [Esterhazy]. Vous avez protesté contre ce crime de lèse-patrie et partagé l'indignation qu'il a soulevé dans le pays tout entier. Pour nous, ministres de paix, nous n'approuvons, certes, ni les violences, ni les cris de mort, car nous sommes de ceux qu'on tue et point de ceux qui tuent; mais pendant qu'on insultait nos généraux nous pensions à la frontière près de laquelle nous sommes nés, et nous sympathisions de tout notre cœur avec ceux qui criaient 'Vive la France! Vive l'Armée!'

MGR MATHIEU: quoted in Agnes Siegfried, *L'Abbé Frémont*, Félix Alcan, 1932, vol. II, p. 112.

3. Moderation: 'L'Univers'

Once a violent intransigent paper under the Second Empire, L'Univers had become increasingly moderate in its support of Catholic interests. Like the vast majority of Catholics, it endorsed the judgment against Dreyfus and defended the army. After the pardon of Dreyfus anticlericalism began to sense its power and accuse the Catholics indiscriminately of anti-Dreyfusard extremism. L'Univers replied with a warning against this simplification. Not all priests or Catholic newspapers, it argues, were extremists, and can it be proved that all Catholics attacked Dreyfus as a Jew rather than as a traitor? Most clergy want social peace not disorder. The government will endanger this very peace if it gives in to the anticlerical demands.

ECLAIRCISSEMENTS

... Il est encore plus fort et plus injuste, il est absolument inique d'étendre à tous les catholiques, à tous les prêtres, tous les religieux, les reproches que pourraient justifier l'attitude et le langage de quelques-un d'entre eux. On me permettra de dire que *l'Univers* compte dans la presse religieuse. Qu'a-t-il fait? Il a trouvé et dit que les conseils de guerre avaient jugé en conscience et avec justice; il a défendu fermement l'armée; il s'est élevé contre les violences des dreyfusards; mais en quoi a-t-il mérité d'être enveloppé dans les accusations dont on frappe injustement toutes les feuilles catholiques? Or d'autres ont fait comme lui.

Et même si nous avions parlé comme ceux que l'on accuse, serait-on autorisé à prétendre que la France catholique a voulu immoler en Dreyfus non un traître mais un juif? Est-ce que les *Semaines religieuses* se sont livrées à des violences de langage et ont blâmé la grâce accordée par 'pitié' qui devait donner la paix et la donnera? Peut-on citer un évêque qui soit intervenu dans ce débat avec colère ou dans un sens quelconque? Certes ils aiment l'armée, nos évêques, et ont foi en sa justice, mais estimant qu'ils n'avaient rien à dire, il n'ont rien dit. Il en a été de même pour le clergé séculier et régulier. Trouverait-on cent prêtres sur cinquante mille qui se soient mêlés à cette lutte? Ils ont prié pour qu'elle cesse au plus tôt comme le voulaient l'intérêt et l'honneur du pays.

Si le gouvernement, complice des sectaires, subit cette pression sous prétexte d'affermir la République, il lui portera un coup plus sensible que ceux qu'elle a reçus jusqu'ici.

EUGÈNE VEUILLOT: *L'Univers et Le Monde*, 10 October 1899.

4. Assertion: Burnichon

For an example of the extremism which L'Univers *states was an exception to the normal Catholic attitude, see the article from* La Croix (*Sources, p. 63, no. 2*) *and the remarks of the clergy who subscribed to the Henry fund* (*Sources, p. 82, no. 2*). *A less violent example of Catholic assertion is provided by the following conclusion of an article on the Jews in France, published in a Jesuit periodical. It has led many historians to agree with Reinach that the Jesuits were the promoters of anti-Dreyfusism and antisemitism. Others have pointed out that this was an isolated article without sequel. Its author was P. J. Burnichon, and although its tone is muted and he states that he has no wish to use the methods of antisemites, its only effect would be to justify the suspicion of Jews held by most Catholics. His main argument is that Jewish power is out of all proportion to their numbers, and the first paragraph is typical of this claim: the Jews control the press. In conclusion, he states a fundamental difference in mentality between Jews and Catholics. Catholics have a tradition of honour which makes money unimportant or less important. But the Jew is a man of money and trade.*

Dans toute l'Europe la plupart des grands journaux qui forment l'opinion sont plus ou moins commandités par les Juifs. C'est ce qui explique, pour le dire en passant, l'attitude de la presse étrangère dans l'affaire Dreyfus.

... De fait, cette race depuis si longtemps établie sur notre sol et mêlée à notre vie reste séparée de nous; et ce n'est pas tant la religion ni les habitudes sociales, ni même les préjugés qui creusent le fossé; c'est bien plutôt son état d'âme, ce qu'on appelle aujourd'hui dans une langue un peu barbare, sa mentalité. Les anthropologistes disaient qu'elle n'a pas le cerveau fait comme le nôtre. L'Israélite a ses défauts et ses qualités comme nous avons les nôtres; mais ses qualités et ses défauts le placent aux antipodes de notre caractère national. Nous avons en particulier dans notre tempérament une certaine disposition où entrent à doses plus ou moins grandes l'esprit chrétien, les traditions de l'honneur, et la légèreté, et qui nous porte à dédaigner l'argent, ou du moins à ne pas en faire aussi grand cas que d'autres... Or, chez nous comme ailleurs, l'Israélite est essentiellement l'homme de l'argent et du trafic...

P. J. BURNICHON: 'La Question du Jour', *Etudes*, 5 December 1898.

5. A Cynical View: Anatole France

In his satirical novel, L'Ile des Pingouins (1908), Anatole France left the positive commitment of the Dreyfusard days (see Sources, p. 23, no. 3) and returned to scepticism and mockery. He portrays the Affair as a ridiculous ferment caused by the theft of 80,000 bales of hay by a man he calls Pyrot (Dreyfus). The Pyrotists (Dreyfusards) have little in common with the Dreyfusists he once admired, and the opponents of Pyrot are treated with caustic humour. In particular, he ridicules in this passage the unquestioning attitude of the clergy. Two priests are in conversation, Agaric and Cornemuse, and the second sets out the necessity of believing in Pyrot's guilt: he could not possibly doubt it, since authority has declared it, and if Pyrot is not condemned because he is guilty, he is guilty because he is condemned. In any case if the judges are wrong it will all be rectified in the next world.

Le pieux Agaric demanda vivement:

— Vous ne doutez pas du crime de Pyrot?

— Je n'en puis douter, très cher Agaric, répondit le religieux des Conils; ce serait contraire aux lois de mon pays, qu'il faut respecter tant qu'elles ne sont pas en opposition avec les lois divines. Pyrot est coupable puisqu'il est condamné. Quant à en dire davantage pour ou contre sa culpabilité, ce serait substituer mon autorité à celle des juges, et je me garderai bien de le faire. C'est ailleurs inutile, puisque Pyrot est condamné. S'il n'est pas condamné parce qu'il est coupable, il est coupable parce qu'il est condamné; cela revient au même. Je crois à sa culpabilité comme tout bon citoyen doit y croire; et j'y croirai tant que la justice établie m'ordonnera d'y croire, car il n'appartient pas à un particulier, mais au juge, de proclamer l'innocence d'un condamné.

La justice humaine est respectable jusque dans les erreurs inhérentes à sa nature faillible et bornée. Ces erreurs ne sont jamais irréparables; si les juges ne les réparent pas sur la terre, Dieu les réparera dans le ciel.

ANATOLE FRANCE: *L'Ile des Pingouins* (1st edn. 1908), Calmann-Lévy, 1925, p. 263.

Anticlericalism

1. Zola's 'Lettre à la France'

Published as a pamphlet, Zola's open warning to France was an article of greater width than J'accuse *which followed it. It did not create the sensation of its successor, but is a better guide to Zola's ideas. This is Zola the conscience of France. Like Gohier (Sources, p. 43, no. 1), he sees the Affair as an incident in the continuous struggle between the Revolution and reaction, between liberty and tyranny. He refers implicitly to Bonapartism, or more recently Boulangism, 'It is a general you want in your bed': dictatorship is near. Even closer is the threat of the Church. Catholicism, he claims, has failed to hold the people. Now it has a golden opportunity to filter back under the cover of antisemitism. By persecuting the Jews it hopes to re-establish its control: it is a subtle process of destroying the resistance of France. Clerical reaction has permeated the Republic (a reference to the Ralliement), but only to kill it from within.*

Mais il est des faits plus graves encore, tout un ensemble de symptômes qui font de la crise que tu traverses, un cas d'une leçon terrifiante, pour ceux qui savent voir et juger. L'Affaire Dreyfus n'est qu'un incident déplorable. L'aveu terrible est la façon dont tu te comportes dans l'aventure. On a l'air bien portant, et tout d'un coup de petites taches apparaissent sur la peau: la mort est en vous. Tout ton empoisonnement politique et social vient de te monter à la face.

... Fais ton examen de conscience: était-ce vraiment ton armée que tu voulais défendre quand personne ne l'attaquait? N'était-ce pas plutôt le sabre que tu avais le brusque besoin d'acclamer? Je vois, pour mon compte, dans la bruyante ovation faite aux chefs qu'on disait insultés, un réveil, inconscient sans doute du boulangisme latent, dont tu restes atteinte. Au fond, tu n'as pas encore le sang républicain, les panaches qui passent te font battre le cœur, un roi ne peut venir sans que tu en tombes amoureuse. Ton armée ah bien! oui tu n'y songes guère. C'est le général que tu veux dans ta couche. Et que l'Affaire Dreyfus est loin! Pendant que le général Billot se faisait acclamer à la chambre, je voyais l'ombre du sabre se dessiner sur la muraille. France si tu ne te méfies, tu vas à la dictature.

Et sais-tu encore où tu vas, France? Tu vas à l'Église, tu retournes au passé, à ce passé d'intolérance et de théocratie, que les plus illustres de tes enfants ont combattu, ont cru tuer, en donnant leur intelligence et leur sang. Aujourd'hui la tactique de l'antisémitisme est bien simple. Vainement le catholicisme s'efforçait d'agir sur le peuple, créait des cercles d'ouvriers, multipliait les pélerinages, échouait à le reconquérir, à le ramener au pied des autels. C'était chose définitive, les églises restaient désertes, le peuple ne croyait plus. Et voilà que des circonstances ont permis de souffler au peuple le rage antisémite, on l'empoisonne de ce fanatisme, on le lance dans les rues criant 'A bas les juifs! à mort les juifs'. Quel triomphe, si l'on pourrait déchaîner une guerre religieuse! Certes le peuple ne croit toujours pas; mais n'est-ce pas le commencement de la croyance que de recommencer l'intolérance du moyen âge, que de faire brûler les juifs en place publique? Enfin voilà donc le poison trouvé, et quand on aura fait du peuple de France un fanatique et un bourreau, quand on lui aura arraché du cœur sa générosité, son amour des droits de l'homme, si durement conquis, Dieu fera sans doute le reste.

On a l'audace de nier la réaction cléricale. Mais elle est partout, elle éclate dans la politique, dans les arts, dans la presse, dans la rue! On persécute aujourd'hui les juifs, ce sera demain le tour des protestants; et déjà la campagne commence. La République est envahie par les réactionnaires de tous genres, ils l'adorent d'un brusque et terrible amour, ils l'embrassent pour l'étouffer. . . .

E. ZOLA: *Lettre à la France*, 6 January 1898.

2. The Henry Fund: Quillard

Of all the anticlerical publications of the Affair, the simple list of subscribers to the Henry fund compiled by Pierre Quillard was one of the most pungent. The names and remarks of the subscribers as they had appeared in La Libre Parole *were reproduced in distinctive categories. From the section marked 'Clergy' the following have been selected. It is easy to imagine the impact which the list made on active or potential anticlericals.*

RELIGIOUS TENSIONS

	Francs	Centimes
Allain (L'abbé) recteur de Plouhan, ex-zouave pontifical	5	—
Collot (L'abbé) Lorrain et prisonnier des Prussiens qui a confiance au jugement de la justice militaire et de cinq ministres de la guerre	5	—
Cros (L'abbé) ex-lieutenant, pour une descente de lit de peau de Youpins, afin de les piétiner matin et soir	5	—
Favier (L'abbé) qui espère que bientôt Dieu vengera la France	5	—
Galey (L'abbé H.) pour la défense du droit éternel contre le cabotinage des puritains et la fourberie judéo-huguenote	5	—
Lamy (E.) prêtre. Pour la défense d'un enfant de France	1	—
Mancuert (Abbé) et M. Gely à Pessac (Gironde) Deux admirateurs de la belle campagne contre nos vrais ennemis	1	20
C. (Abbé) Le sang du colonel Henry crie vengeance	3	—
E.B. Paris. Un prêtre convaincu de la perversité des Juifs	0	50
Un curé de campagne, qui fait les vœux les plus ardents pour l'extermination des deux ennemis de la France: le Juif et le Franc-Maçon	5	—
Un curé de diocèse de Bayeux. A bas les républicains de tout acabit: Youpins, huguenots, francs-maçons et tous les enjuivés comme eux	1	—
Un petit curé poitevin qui chanterait avec plaisir le Requiem du dernier des Youpins	1	—
Trois curés, Français de France (Mauriennais) qui voudraient appliquer leurs trente doigts sur la figure immonde du Juif Reinach	3	—

PIERRE QUILLARD: *Le Monument Henry*, Stock 1899.

3. The Jesuit Plot: Reinach

Throughout the Affair the Dreyfusard writings of Joseph Reinach form a commentary on the beliefs and progress of the revisionists. He was a man of dogmatic opinions without being a fanatic. The Affair was his life, and his History of the Affair his life's work. Written between 1900 and 1908, it reproduces most of the opinions he held in the thick of the Affair and in particular his accusations against the Jesuits and Père du Lac. Although he met du Lac at a dinner party and heard the Jesuit's denials, he refused to reconsider his charges. Throughout this passage he imputes the most subtle of methods and the basest of motives to the Jesuits. They act, he states, secretly and silently: they have made the so-called crime of Dreyfus into the crime of all Jews; they represent the powers of dogma and illiberalism (The Syllabus of Errors, 1864). *By slow infiltration they have made their way into all corners of society and established a firm hold over their pupils. They use the confessional for their insidious purposes. And behind them lurks the figure of Père du Lac.*

C'est la politique, la méthode, l'art, vraiment admirable, de la Société de Jésus, d'agir, le plus souvent, sans se montrer. A travers tant d'événements qu'elle a conduits depuis quatre siècles, surtout depuis la fin de l'ancien Régime, on la sent, si je puis dire; on ne la voit pas.

Il en avait été de même, jusqu'à présent, dans l'histoire que je raconte. Partout, le même genre d'action, la même méthode se manifeste. Mais le moteur n'apparaît point.

Du premier jour où éclata la tragédie, la Société l'avait suivie avec une attention soutenue, et avait découvert, d'un œil qui voit loin, l'immense parti qu'elle en pourrait tirer: faire du crime d'un seul le crime de toute une race, 'le fond du Juif étant la trahison, la fourberie et le mensonge'; puis, cette première barrière renversée, submerger sous le même flot 'les alliés' des juifs, protestants et francs-maçons, tous les fils de l'Encyclopédie. Et ce sera la victoire du *Syllabus*, qui dit anathème à la liberté de conscience, la revanche de l'Eglise contre la Révolution, que ce soit sous un roi ou quelque Césarion restauré, ou sous une République plus misérable que la plus faible des Monarchies.

... Cependant, il serait excessif de tout rapporter aux Jésuites. Ce serait tomber dans leur mensonge favori: tout rapporter aux Juifs, aux francs-maçons. Dans l'Eglise même, il y eut, comme sous la Ligue, d'autres foyers d'intrigues et d'action. Les grossiers assomptionnistes, qui ont succédé aux capucins d'autrefois (les 'chiens des jésuites'), les dominicains, véhéments ou subtils, des curés populaires ou mondains (celui de Sainte-Clotilde, à Paris) auraient, comme les théatins ou les carmes d'autrefois, 'le droit de réclamer'. Toutefois, la grande inspiration profonde, c'est celle du Gésu.

Depuis un quart de siècle, par une lente infiltration, les Pères se sont emparés de l'éducation des classes riches, aisées. Ils ont préparé des générations pour les grandes écoles (navale, militaires); leurs élèves, ayant depuis peu l'âge d'homme, sont partout, dans les professions libérales, avocats et médecins, à la tête de la grande industrie, du grand commerce. L'Université, quand elle a formé ses bacheliers, ne les connaît plus. Eux, jamais ne lâchent les élèves dont ils ont façonné le cerveau, pétri le cœur; ils les suivent dans la vie, les poussent, les marient. Dans toutes les carrières, même administratives, surtout dans l'armée, être recommandé (secrètement), soutenu par les Pères, c'est un avantage sans prix. Et ce qui échappe à l'éducation, à cette tutelle prolongée le confessional le leur ramène. Peu à peu, dans le beau monde aristocratique et le monde bourgeois qui 'pense bien', le jésuite a remplacé, comme directeur, les autres moines, le simple prêtre, bon pour les petites gens. Il pénètre ainsi au secret des familles, documente une immense agence d'informations.

Partout des milliers d'obligés, de fidèles, attendent, pour le colporter, le mot d'ordre, qui vient de la petite cellule du père Du Lac, si simple, un crucifix sur le mur nu, et, sur la table de travail, toujours ouvert et annoté, l'*Annuaire*.

J. REINACH: *Histoire de l'Affaire Dreyfus*, vol. III, *La Crise*, Fasquelle, 1903, pp. 22-6.

4. An English Version: Conybeare

Reinach's theory of the Jesuit plot made its way to England through another anticlerical Yves Guyot, editor of Le Siècle. Here it was completely accepted by an Oxford historian Frederick Cornwallis, who was deeply interested in the Affair. Under the name Fred Conybeare he wrote The Dreyfus Case, *the first English treatment, and of considerable influence on succeeding English historians of the Affair. In his conclusion he sums up the case against the Jesuits.*

Thus a larger problem awaits the French than the mere rehabilitation of Dreyfus and the retrieving of their national character, so sorely tarnished in the last two years. They must reform the army itself and insist on the officers being law-abiding and really loyal to the institutions they have sworn to defend. The first step will be to emancipate the army from the Jesuits who have fastened their teeth into it: and this can be done by enforcing the decrees of 1880 and so obliging the

Jesuits to quit France. We hope that no more of them will drift into England. Secondly the Jesuit military schools in the Rue des Postes and elsewhere must be closed and a law made that no young men shall be admitted into St Cyr and the Polytechnique who have not been educated up to the moment of their admission in the national lycées, which are not confessional schools. Thirdly the state must look after the military clubs provided for the common soldier, and see that they are not mere centres of Jesuit propaganda, where such sheets as those of MM. Maurras, Drumont and Judet are alone set before him. . . .

FRED C. CONYBEARE: *The Dreyfus Case*, London, George Allen, 1898, p. 317.

5. The Venom of Anticlericalism: Ajalbert

Jean Ajalbert, a writer of popular pamphlets and books against the church, saw clericalism as incurably evil. This extract is typical of his method. He evokes a pleasant picture of bells ringing across towns, villages and countryside and then shatters it ruthlessly: the bells become the clanging of hate, the chime of clerical materialism.

Cependant ô prêtres, les cloches s'ébranlent joyeuses, par le radieux été, au-dessus des villes accablées, des clairs villages, des landes sèches, des bois frais, des moissons blondes, le matin, le soir de tous les jours, et tout le jour des dimanches et des fêtes.

Est-ce qu'elles appellent pour la justice? Non. Elles sont, ces cloches, comme les canons, d'un bronze impitoyable. Leur carillon ne vibre que pour la haine: le plus souvent, et quand elles célèbrent baptêmes et mariages, ou se lamentent d'un cadavre, elles distinguent entre le pauvre et le riche; elles n'en sonnent que pour l'argent.

JEAN AJALBERT: *La Forêt noire*, 1899, p. iv.

Catholic Dreyfusards

1. Abbé Frémont

A well-known Paris preacher, the Abbé Frémont was one of the most outspoken Catholic Dreyfusards. To Mgr Mathieu he wrote, 'Believe me it is not Catholicism itself that I accuse; I do not make the puerile confusion of doctrine and people which is common at the moment, but I feel certain that Catholics bear an enormous responsibility. But who dares to tell them?' He himself did not hesitate to do so, but he often despaired of making any impact. In this letter to a friend he bemoans the blindness of Catholics in the world of political realism.

... Le procès Dreyfus, qui s'illumine si tragiquement aux éclairs du coup de rasoir de Henry, est une preuve de plus de notre légèreté et de notre passion. Pourquoi la presse pseudo-catholique a-t-elle pris parti pour Henry, et Boisdeffre et les autres? Uniquement parce qu'il s'agissait d'écraser un Juif.

La République est plus solide que jamais, et les Catholiques ont tort de ne pas se jeter dans la mêlée pour soutenir le drapeau de la démocratie: ils seraient bientôt tout puissants. Mais nous n'avons pas le génie politique; la chose est sûre, et c'est à peine si nous commençons à comprendre que '89 est une réalité.

ABBÉ FRÉMONT to his friend Fouruchon, 19 September 1898: in Agnes Siegfried, *L'Abbé Frémont*, Félix Alcan, 1932, vol. II, p. 166.

2. Abbé Brugerette

The aims and limitations of the Catholic Dreyfusards are presented in this passage. Abbé Brugerette ascribed the anti-Dreyfusism of most Catholics to their lack of critical faculties. Deadened by obedience and submission, they failed to enquire beyond their own Catholic newspapers. But, he states here, not all Catholics were blind. A small number tried to enlighten their fellow believers and distract them from their worship of the army. The Catholic committee founded for this purpose ran parallel to other Dreyfusism (meaning the Ligue des Droits de l'Homme) by basing its principles on those of 1789. This alliance was a totally new phenomenon. But the efforts of the Catholic Dreyfusards, he concludes, came to nothing: they had no influence, and even certain large papers with Catholic leanings failed to move their public. So what could their small group accomplish?

Le crime collectif d'intolérance ne fut pas cependant le crime de tous. Dans cette nuit profonde qui nous voila l'image de plus simples vérités, au milieu de ce déchaînement de toutes les forces d'ignorance et de mensonge quelques-uns des nôtres surent fermer l'oreille aux doctrines de haine: et, revêtus seulement des armes de la charité et de la raison, ils osèrent braver les pires avanies pour faire entendre une chrétienne protestation contre les crimes commis au nom de la justice. Ils voulurent apporter des paroles de paix et de vérité à leurs frères égarés, les convaincre qu'il ne suffit pas d'avoir des galons pour planer au-dessus de toutes les erreurs, les mettre en garde contre les déclamations virulentes d'une presse pharisaïque qui traînait après elle afin d'éblouir les yeux, tous les clinquants et les oripeaux ramassés dans le vestiaire des sacristies et la garde-robe des états-majors. Ils voulurent enfin élever en terre d'Église le 'temple de sagesse et de vérité', dont parle le poète antique et qui devait servir d'asile à toutes les consciences désireuses de se libérer, à toutes les énergies impatientes de s'employer à la défense de la justice.

Ces hommes furent les catholiques dreyfusards, ce temple de justice fut le Comité catholique pour la défense du Droit.

... Par ses principes et par son but, le Comité catholique tendait à la conciliation sur le terrain des faits, de ces prétendues antinomies qui s'appellent la foi chrétienne et la pensée moderne, l'autorité et la liberté. Son credo c'était en effet, le libre examen politique, et c'est au nom de ce libre examen qu'il affermait et croyait pouvoir défendre l'innocence de l'officier juif. Le Dreyfusisme confessionnel allait donc parallèlement au même but que le Dreyfusisme laïque. Comme lui encore, il dénonçait le mal profond causé au pays par le militarisme, l'antisémitisme et le nationalisme. Comme lui enfin il déclarait 's'appuyer sur les principes de 1789' pour le triomphe définitif de la justice et de la vérité dans la crise actuelle. Et les actes, cette fois, étaient la traduction littérale des principes. Ils étaient la répudiation sans équivoque de cléricalisme.

... On avait vu à la fin du XIXe siècle ce fait insolite, peut-être unique: des catholiques, des libres-penseurs, des protestants et des juifs, marchant la main dans la main pour le même idéal de justice et de vérité.

... [Mais] les efforts généreux du Dreyfusisme catholique restèrent cependant stériles. Lui aussi vit attristé et impuissant la débâcle de ses espoirs perdus. Ses moyens furent d'ailleurs trop au-dessous du but poursuivi. Pour réaliser son magnifique idéal de liberté, pour porter chez ses amis comme chez ses ennemis la bonne parole de justice et de paix, *verbum pacis et justitiae*, le Comité catholique pour la défense du Droit n'avait même un journal hebdomadaire. Il fut d'ailleurs à peine connu du monde religieux. Car c'était et c'est toujours la tactique de la presse nationaliste et cléricale de laisser ignorer à ses lecteurs qu'il pouvait et qu'il peut encore exister des catholiques et des prêtres dreyfusards.

Telle est toutefois la profondeur des préjugés enracinés dans notre mentalité qu'il est permis de se demander si même en inondant le pays catholique de ses journaux et de ses brochures, le Comité pour la défense du Droit aurait vraiment réussi à faire remonter le courant d'hostilité à l'œuvre de justice et de vérité. *Le Figaro, le Soleil, l'Autorité* avaient été impuissants à ouvrir les yeux de leurs lecteurs à la lumière de la raison et de la vérité. Toute autre tentative dans le même sens semblait donc condamnés d'avance...

ABBÉ H. DE SAINT-POLI (Abbé J. Brugerette): *L'Affaire Dreyfus et la mentalité catholique en France*, Storck, 1904, pp. 177–88.

IV
Political Tensions

The arrest and conviction of Dreyfus seized the imagination of the public. At the time of Boulanger in 1889 it had been apparent that public opinion, especially in Paris, was nationalist and chauvinistic. The image of a general who would stir the government into an assertive anti-Germanism was a popular one. It is therefore not surprising that Dreyfus was insulted by a hostile crowd at his degradation, nor that the army stood high in public esteem for its exposure and conviction of the traitor.

In the chamber of deputies the government of Charles Dupuy also willingly endorsed the judgment against Dreyfus. It was a government of moderate republicans, conservative in social policy, protectionist in economics; the republican bourgeois élite as Sorel later called them. They supported the Pope's policy of rallying the Catholics to the Republic and appeared to have established, for the first time in the Third Republic, a viable conservative republican bloc in the chamber. To their left lay the Radicals, who, as guardians of republican anti-clericalism, were critical of the Ralliement. Beyond the Radicals sat the Socialist groups, who pursued an independent line, committed neither to the Republic as it was then constructed, nor to its internal and foreign policies. They were heavily scornful of the republican élite, since it refused to tackle the social problems which kept the working class in an inferior, underprivileged position. To the right of the government were the small bands of political conservatives who, to varying degrees, repudiated the whole idea of the Republic, looking instead to a new régime based perhaps on a reinstated monarchy.

In its delicately balanced position the government was careful to avoid any crisis which would threaten its existence. For this reason its initial support for the conviction of Dreyfus had to be maintained. The conviction had been popular, the army court-martial had been unanimous, and there seemed to be no reason to take seriously the complaints of the early revisionists. They were only a small handful of men, most of whom, as friends of Dreyfus or sympathising Jews, could be held as personally biased. The hostile treatment of political circles towards Scheurer-Kestner's campaign showed the unwillingness of politicians to provoke the storm which revision would have entailed. Nor were the political opponents of the government prepared to do so. They began in fact by criticising the sentence as too lenient: Dreyfus, they argued, was given preferential treatment as one of the republican élite, and the right wing of the chamber continued throughout the Affair to call for harsh measures against Dreyfus and his supporters. The Socialists were at first equally hostile to revision, which they diagnosed as the bourgeois machinations of capitalist Jews, but as the revisionist campaign increased in 1897 they withdrew into a position of strategic neutrality, calling the proletariat to abstain from a purely bourgeois conflict in which two aspects of capitalist decadence, Judaism and Clericalism, battled for the spoils.[1]

The politicians, therefore, were not responsible for the eruption of ideas and emotions which made the Affair and which began to divide French opinion at the end of 1897. This achievement was almost entirely the work of journalists, men of ideas and those like Scheurer-Kestner and Jean Jaurès who were exceptions to the general political caution.[2]

The chamber's opposition to revision continued well into 1898. It decreed that Zola should be prosecuted for his accusations; Méline, the prime minister from 1896 to 1898, denied categorically that the Dreyfus Affair even existed, and General Cavaignac, war minister in the cabinet formed after the May elections, claimed that he had indisputable proof of the guilt of Dreyfus.

The public also continued its anti-Dreyfusism. A hostile crowd at Zola's trial shouted and threatened violence against the man who had dared to accuse the nation's army of corruption. The reputation of the great novelist was of no account when weighed against the apparent antipatriotism of his accusing article. Similarly the majority of the nation's electorate declared themselves either indifferent or hostile to revision when they went to the polls in May 1898. Jaurès was defeated; Clemenceau did not even attempt to regain the seat he had lost after Panama, whereas the vitriolic Drumont was overwhelmingly returned in antisemitic Algeria. The chamber which met after these elections declared at once its intention to stand by the judgment of 1894. Despite Scheurer-Kestner's and Lazare's discoveries, despite Zola's

[1] See Sources, p. 99, Socialist Manifesto.
[2] For the political views of Jaurès during the Affair, see Sources, p. 103, no. 2.

J'accuse, despite the suspicious past of Esterhazy, the attitude of politicians had not changed. Revision was seen as a dangerous issue, one to be excluded from politics in order to prevent a constitutional crisis which might throw the Republic into confusion.

Although the elections had brought no party of convinced Dreyfusards to the chamber, they were not of insignificance for the Affair. Since the 1870s when the régime was disputed between republicans and monarchists, the majority of the electorate had shown itself more and more republican in sympathy. It supported the legislation against Catholics and monarchists, whom they saw as a threat to the Republic, and in the elections of 1892 had given little backing to the idea of the Ralliement. The Affair did nothing to change the republicanism and anticlericalism of this electorate: it merely grafted on to these existing attitudes the anti-Dreyfusard convictions which seemed so obviously patriotic. Thus in the elections of 1898 the majority of voters returned anti-Dreyfusards who were also republicans and anticlericals. They had no difficulty in finding such candidates, since the republican politicians had made little attempt to embrace the Dreyfusard cause.

But the importance of the elections was not so much that they returned anti-Dreyfusards but that they returned a majority of anticlericals or men who for other reasons wished to end the Ralliement. Méline's government fell and the new government of Brisson was a Radical one. Thus the centre of political gravity in the chamber had shifted to the left. This shift was crucial. Where before, the government of Méline in its policy of reconciliation with the Catholics had claimed that Dreyfusism was the major threat to the constitution, the new government, made up of Radicals and anticlericals, came gradually to realise that the threat lay not in revisionism but in the clericalism and nationalism of the anti-Dreyfusards. The politics of 1898–99 are the history of this conversion of the political left to Dreyfusism. Two major factors pushed them in this direction. Firstly, Henry's suicide, which threw doubt on the whole Army case against Dreyfus, and secondly, the assertiveness of the revaluated nationalism which, inspired by Maurras and adopted by extremist clericals and antisemites, threatened the Revolutionary tradition of France.

Acute political tensions were suddenly revealed. As the political left in the chamber veered round to revision and the government began to sympathise with the Dreyfusard campaign, so the anti-Dreyfusards, deserted by the Republic, began to talk in terms of a new régime.

Maurras continued to develop his monarchist ideology;[1] *La Croix* became antirepublican; Déroulède, although himself a republican, massed his Ligue des Patriotes for a showdown with the treacherous politicians. The climax came in February 1899 with the death of President Faure. The President had been a staunch anti-Dreyfusard, and his death while entertaining his mistress in his private office did little to help the public image of his opinions. His successor, President Loubet, was known to be sympathetic to revision. It seemed to the nationalists that the régime had finally gone over to the enemy. The situation produced farcical desperation. On 23 February 1899 at the funeral procession for Félix Faure, Déroulède failed to drag a stolid army officer into the Elysée palace as a prelude to a coup d'état. He had mistaken his man. General Roget had no pretensions to political power. In June the *opéra bouffe* continued when a nationalist, Baron Christiani, assaulted Loubet at the Auteuil races, knocking the President's top hat to the ground with a patriotic gesture. The left-wing republicans of the chamber were finally convinced that the Republic was in jeopardy. On 24 June 1899 a new ministry under Waldeck-Rousseau pledged itself to establish a new republican solidarity; the first step in the succession of events which led to the formation of a left-wing bloc (Bloc des Gauches) and the anticlerical ministry of Combes. Dreyfusism had become firmly political. The Revolutionary tradition, which it had embodied outside the chamber in Lazare, Clemenceau, Zola and Jaurès, was finally vindicated and expressed within the chamber by the governments of Waldeck-Rousseau and Combes. Most significantly a portion of socialist opinion had rallied to the republican government. In Waldeck-Rousseau's cabinet Millerand, as Minister of Commerce, was the first European socialist to hold ministerial office and behind the Combist legislation was the strong support of Jaurès.

The more immediate consequence of the new republican formation in 1899 was the acceleration of revision. Dreyfus was brought back to France and his retrial set in motion. The second conviction of Rennes would therefore appear to be a defiance of the government. In fact, the government was not perturbed: had Dreyfus been declared innocent at Rennes the government might have been forced to prosecute his army accusers or to look for the real traitor. With the Paris Exhibition scheduled for 1900 there was every incentive to close the Affair. On 19 September 1899 Dreyfus was pardoned; Scheurer-

[1] See Sources, p. 107, no. 1, Maurras.

Kestner died on the same day. The revisionists had their moral victory; the army retained its honour. The Third Republic had survived its most serious crisis.

The consolidation of left-wing politicians which had secured its survival is a phenomenon of all the major crises in French political history since 1870. Its recurrence is sufficiently regular to allow illustration by a model situation. The republican government is first threatened from groups on the right and on the left of the chamber. As the crisis develops it becomes apparent that not merely the government but the Republic itself is endangered. At this point the criticism from the left weakens and a process of republican consolidation on the left sets in, making the crisis into a dualistic one, left against right. In this process the former critics on the left rally to the Republic and a vacuum is created in which more extreme left-wing critics arise.

To see the particular events from which this model has been built one can turn to the 1870s when the Third Republic in its initial stages was criticised from the left by the party of Gambetta and from the right by the monarchists. When the monarchist threat increased Gambetta rallied to the Republic and its survival was secured. In the 1880s his place on the left was taken by Clemenceau, a more extreme Radical critic, but in the crisis over Boulanger, Clemenceau came to support the Republic against its Boulangist opponents on the right. He was succeeded by the Socialists who, by the time of the Affair, had entered the chamber on the extreme left and were hostile to the Republic as it existed in the 1890s. But in 1899 some of them, though not all, were drawn into the new left-wing solidarity to defend the Third Republic against the nationalists. In turn their places on the extreme left were taken by the Communists in the 1920s, but in the struggle against Fascism even they rallied to the Republic, firstly in the formation of the Popular Front in 1936, and secondly, during the Resistance; and after the Second World War they took part for a short while in the Liberation government, a concession to the Western parliamentary system which was soon retracted as the Cold War began. Since then they have returned to their rôle as the extreme critics on the left.

Thus the Bloc des Gauches has made itself felt at several critical moments in recent French history, and there is talk among present left-wing opponents of de Gaulle of its continuing potential. But in tracing a recurrent political phenomenon there is no implication that the crises were identical. Each had its own particularities, and in 1899 it was the particular events of the Affair, not the power of a recurrent pattern, which induced Millerand to sit in the cabinet and Jaurès to support the policies of Waldeck-Rousseau and Combes. There were, on the other hand, Socialists of the Guèsde school who remained hostile to this development just as they had remained neutral during the Affair, and this is a reminder of the complexity which must be acknowledged whenever a generalisation has been advanced.

SOURCES

Deputies and the Affair

1. Unity

At the time of this session in the Chamber of Deputies, the Affair had not yet divided France and politicians were vying with each other in patriotic gestures. But various accusations against the army leaders were beginning to spread. Against one such accusation General Boisdeffre, Chief of the General Staff, pinned a notice of protest on the doors of the Chamber. When questioned about this the prime minister Méline finally remarked, 'There is no Dreyfus Affair'. Albert de Mun, an ex-officer and the celebrated founder of Catholic circles for working men, was not satisfied. With a defiant speech he demands the attendance of the minister of war, General Billot. The honour of France and the army, he declares, is in question: only Billot can fully vindicate the reputation of Boisdeffre. He claims that the issue transcends party differences and touches the very root of the nation. De Mun was applauded by most of the deputies. Only later did it become significant that one of the most eloquent Catholic politicians had thrown his influence behind the army and against revision.

De Mun: C'est à lui, en effet, que mon interpellation s'adresse, parce que c'est à lui, c'est au chef du département de la guerre que je veux demander de venir ici, par une parole solennelle, venger les chefs de l'armée (*vifs applaudissements à droite, à l'extrême-gauche et à gauche*) et en particulier le chef de l'état-major général. (*Nouveaux applaudissements sur les mêmes bancs.*)

Il est indispensable que cette tâche gouvernementale soit remplie, et soit remplie par celui qui a qualité pour parler au nom de l'armée. Il faut qu'on sache s'il est vrai qu'il y ait dans ce pays une puissance mystérieuse et occulte (*nouveaux applaudissements*) assez forte pour pouvoir à son gré jeter le soupçon sur ceux qui commandent à notre armée, sur ceux qui, le jour où de grands devoirs s'imposeront à elle, auront mission de la conduire à l'ennemi et de diriger la guerre. (*Applaudissements.*) Il faut qu'on sache si cette puissance occulte est vraiment assez forte pour bouleverser le pays tout entier, comme il l'est depuis plus de quinze jours, pour jeter dans les esprits le doute et le soupçon contre des officiers qui ... (*vifs applaudissements*).

Ah! Vous demandez qu'il n'y eût pas ici de question politique: non, il n'y en a pas! (*Nouveaux applaudissements sur un grand nombre de bancs.*)

Il n'y a ici ni amis, ni adversaires, ni ministériels, ni ennemis du cabinet: il y a des représentants du pays, il y a des Français soucieux de conserver intact ce qu'ils ont de plus précieux, ce qui reste, au milieu de nos luttes et de nos discordes de parti le terrain commun de nos invincibles espérances: l'honneur de l'armée. (*Vifs applaudissements.*)

Non, il n'y a pas de question politique: il y a un Français, représentant de son pays, qui a servi sa patrie sous les armes pendant quinze ans et dont le cœur de soldat est remué jusqu'au fond par l'odieuse campagne à laquelle nous assistons. (*Applaudissements.*)

Je demande que M. le ministre de la Guerre—et ce n'est trop exiger—vienne ici pour s'associer à mes paroles, pour exprimer hautement ses sentiments qui sont dans son cœur, j'en suis sûr, comme dans le mien. Je demande qu'il parle, afin que nous ne soyons pas réduits à voir le chef de l'état-major général de l'armée obligé de sortir de sa réserve militaire pour faire afficher à la porte au lieu de vos séances ... (*Applaudissements sur un grand nombre de bancs.*)

M. *René Goblet:* C'est l'anarchie par le Gouvernement!

M. *le Comte Albert de Mun* ... pour faire afficher là un démenti contre ceux qui l'accusent de pactiser avec des hommes accusés de trahison.

Comment! cette lettre vient d'être affichée à votre porte et M. le ministre de la Guerre n'est pas ici, lui qui peut parler à la tribune pour venger l'armée outragée. (*Applaudissements sur les mêmes bancs.*)

Ce n'est pas possible! Il faut qu'il parle.

J'ai dit ce que j'avais à dire, j'espère que les membres du Gouvernement, immédiatement par les moyens qu'ils ont à leur disposition, vont faire connaître à M. le ministre de la Guerre l'émotion qui s'empare de la Chambre et qu'ils le prieront de venir ici donner satisfaction aux sentiments qui agitent les cœurs de tous les patriotes. (*Applaudissements prolongés à gauche, à l'extrême-gauche et à la droite.*)

Journal Officiel, 4 December 1897.

2. Division

The passionate exchange of insults and blows which Jaurès provoked in this session was the first sign of major division within the chamber, though the numbers who supported the socialist leader were small. Not long before this speech he had signed the Manifesto reproduced later in this section (p. 99), but since then he had become committed to the Dreyfusard cause. His revised attitude can be seen in the article printed on p. 103 (no. 2). In this conclusion to a violent attack on the prosecutors of Zola he states that there has been nothing but mystery and lies throughout the whole Affair. Zola had been charged not for the complete assertions of J'accuse *but on one small detail, which thus kept the trial away from the controversial aspects of the Dreyfus judgment. A shout from a right-wing deputy begins the stream of insults, and the action of one of Jaurès's supporters begins the brawl. In chaos the session is suspended. Jaurès had brought Dreyfusism to the chamber, but in the minds of many the spectre of the Jewish syndicate gained substance.*

Jaurès ... C'est assez des habilités; c'est assez et trop des équivoques. (*Applaudissements à l'extrême-gauche.*) Savez-vous ce dont nous souffrons à l'heure présente? (*A droite*—De vous.)

Savez-vous ce dont nous mourons tous? Je le dis sous la responsabilité de ma conscience personnelle: nous mourons tous, depuis que cette affaire est ouverte, des demi-mesures, des réticences, des équivoques, des mensonges, des lâchetés. (*Vifs applaudissements à l'extrême-gauche.*)

Oui des équivoques, des mensonges, des lâchetés. (*Vifs applaudissements répétés à l'extrême-gauche et sur divers bancs à gauche.*)

Il y a d'abord, quoi que vous avez fait pour en atténuer le scandale, il y a mensonge et lâcheté dans les poursuites incomplètes dirigées contre Zola. (*Vifs applaudissements à l'extrême-gauche et sur divers bancs à gauche*—*Protestations au centre et à droite.*)

(*Voix nombreuses au centre*—A l'ordre. A l'ordre!)

M. le Président: M. Jaurès, pour cette parole, je vous rappelle formellement à l'ordre. (*Applaudissements.*)

Esterhazy Ier! Pourquoi pas?..

From the Dreyfusard *Le Sifflet*, 17 February 1898

M. le Président du Conseil: Si nous disions des choses pareilles on verrait quelles tempêtes nous soulèverions de ce côté (*l'extrême-gauche*). (Très bien! Très bien! *au centre.*)

M. Jaurès: Il vous était possible—et nous vous le demandions—de ne pas exercer de poursuites, parce que le huis clos, tout au moins, a besoin de ce correctif nécessaire de la critique au dehors. (*Exclamations au centre et à droite.*)

Mais enfin, puisque vous vous décidiez à poursuivre, puisque vous portiez ce document au jury pour que le jury décidât et jugeât, de quel droit, en vertu de quel principe, avez-vous fait un choix entre les diverses parties de cet article? (*Applaudissements à l'extrême-gauche et sur quelques bancs à gauche.—Bruit au centre.*)

INCIDENT

M. le Comte de Bernis: Vous êtes du Syndicat? (*Vives interruptions à l'extrême-gauche.*)

M. Jaurès: Que dites-vous M. de Bernis?

M. le Comte de Bernis: Je dis que vous devez être du Syndicat, que vous êtes probablement l'avocat du Syndicat!

M. Jaurès: M. de Bernis vous êtes un misérable et un lâche! (*Vifs applaudissements à l'extrême-gauche—Exclamations prolongées au centre, à gauche et à droite—Vive agitation.*)

(*M. Gérault-Richard traverse l'hémicycle, s'élance sur M. de Bernis et le frappe—Tumulte prolongé.*)

M. le Président lève la séance.

[After which M. de Bernis hit Jaurès twice on the neck as he was descending the tribune.]

Journal Officiel, 22 January 1898.

Socialist Neutralism

The Socialist deputies had begun by using the Affair in the chamber as a weapon with which to challenge the government. They had accused the Republic of negligence, then of favouritism for its 'leniency' towards Dreyfus. But as the Affair gathered impetus outside parliament and the press began its polemical warfare it seemed to the socialists that the quarrel was merely a bourgeois struggle for power and influence within a capitalistic régime. The manifesto presents this conviction—one which Jules Guèsde and Vaillant *continued to hold, but one which Jaurès and Millerand soon rejected. It begins with a demand for an open examination of the Affair and proceeds to accuse the Opportunists (the conservative republicans in power at the time) and the clericals of using the Affair to exploit the people and eliminate true democracy. The clericals, it continues, are using antisemitism against all their enemies in order to gain France for themselves, while the Jewish capitalists are promoting their own interests and those of their republican allies. In this situation the proletariat while defending justice for every individual will not be duped by the lies and hypocrisy of the conflict. They must keep themselves free to pursue their own struggle for the Socialist Republic.*

MANIFESTE DES DÉPUTÉS SOCIALISTES AU PROLÉTARIAT

Citoyens,

Depuis que l'agitation se développe autour de l'Affaire Dreyfus, l'obscurité s'épaissit sans cesse et les hommes de bonne foi cherchent péniblement leur route. Avant tout le prolétariat socialiste a besoin de clarté. Sur le fond même de l'Affaire Dreyfus nous n'avons pas qualité pour nous prononcer. Dans la société d'aujourd'hui où tant de forces s'exercent contre la vérité et le droit, il nous est impossible de reconnaître, en principe, l'autorité de la chose jugée; mais nous n'avons aucune raison particulière de repousser ou de respecter au fond les jugements particuliers rendus dans cette affaire. Avant-hier encore nous soutenions de notre vote un ancien ministre de la guerre qui réclamait la production immédiate d'un document capable, selon lui, de confondre d'un coup les défenseurs de Dreyfus et d'établir la culpabilité de celui-ci.

C'est la majorité ministérielle, majorité de centre et de droite qui s'y est opposée. Pour nous, sans parti sur le fond des choses, nous ne réclamons que la lumière.

Pourquoi donc l'Affaire Dreyfus a-t-elle pris des proportions si vastes? C'est qu'elle est devenue le champ de combat des deux factions rivales de la classe bourgeoise, des deux clans bourgeois: les opportunistes et les cléricaux. Opportunistes et cléricaux sont d'accord pour duper et mater la démocratie. Ils sont d'accord pour tenir le peuple en tutelle, pour écraser les syndicats ouvriers, pour prolonger par tous les moyens le régime capitaliste et le salariat et pour assurer à une classe privilégiée, la leur, l'exploitation effrénée du travail et du budget.

Mais ils se querellent pour le partage des bénéfices sociaux et ils se disputent l'exploitation de la République et du peuple, comme ces clans barbares qui s'entendent pour piller et qui se battent ensuite autour du butin. L'Affaire Dreyfus a fourni aux deux clans le prétexte du combat. D'un côté les cléricaux, brusquement rapprochés du pouvoir par la trahison des républicains, tournent autour des places et des émoluments avec une convoitise aiguisée par quinze ans de jeûne. Ils voudraient exploiter la sentence de trahison rendue contre un juif pour disqualifier tous les juifs, et avec eux, tous les dissidents, protestants ou libres-penseurs. Ils écarteraient ainsi tous leurs rivaux des hautes fonctions, administratives et judiciaires, des hauts emplois, des hauts grades, des hauts traitements, et la France serait livrée aussi à cette noblesse chrétienne famélique et décavée qui courtise les juifs, parade à leurs fêtes, danse à leurs bals, emprunte à leurs caisses et, entre deux valses et deux emprunts médite d'étrangler avec un nœud de corde sa dette et son créancier.

Tous ces hommes, détournant les mots de leur sens vraiment national, crient 'La France aux Français'. Cela signifie pour eux 'La France à nous et à nous seuls! Toute la proie pour nos dents longues!' Voilà la tactique, voilà l'intérêt des cléricaux bourgeois. De l'autre côté les capitalistes juifs, après tous les scandales qui les ont discrédités ont besoin pour garder leur part de butin de se réhabiliter un peu. S'ils pouvaient démontrer à propos d'un des leurs qu'il y a erreur judiciaire et violence du préjugé public, ils chercheraient, dans cette réhabilitation directe d'un individu de leur clan et d'accord avec leurs alliés opportunistes, la réhabilitation indirecte de tout le groupe judaïsant et panamisant.

Ils iraient laver à cette fontaine toutes les souillures d'Israël. Et de même que les cléricaux couvrent d'un beau zèle patriotique et national leurs misérables convoitises, les opportunistes et judaïsants s'essayent à une résolution politique et morale en invoquant le droit sacré de la défense, les garanties légales dues à tout homme. Belles paroles et belle doctrine! Certes, le prolétariat qui doit défendre à la fois ses hauts intérêts de classe et le patrimoine de la civilisation humaine qu'il gérera demain, ne doit pas être insensible à l'injustice, même si elle frappe un membre de la classe ennemie.

Non, il n'y est pas insensible, mais il n'est pas dupe.

... Dans la lutte convulsive des deux factions bourgeoises rivales tout est hypocrisie, tout est mensonge. Ils mentent, les cléricaux, quand ils appellent patriotisme leur honteux appétit des places et des traitements. Ils mentent, les opportunistes quand ils invoquent, pour se sauver, le droit humain violé par eux, la veille contre vous.

Haut les cœurs citoyens, au-dessus de cette ignominieuse mêlée. Prolétaires, ne vous enrôlez dans aucun des clans de cette guerre civile bourgeoise. Ne vous livrez pas à ces possédants, rivaux d'un jour, commensaux du même privilège, convives échauffés et gloutons qui se prennent de querelle dans le banquet et qui demain se réconcilieront contre vous si vous forcez la porte de la salle.

Entre Reinach et de Mun gardez votre liberté entière... Citoyens. Sus à vos ennemis, à tous vos ennemis! Ne vous laissez pas diviser par des mots d'ordre incomplets et contradictoires. Poussez votre triple cri de guerre: Guerre au capital juif ou chrétien, guerre au cléricalisme, guerre à l'oligarchie militaire.

... Contre le capital, le Dogme et le Sabre, groupez-vous et combattez en pleine clarté pour la République sociale!

[Signed by 32 socialist deputies including: Guèsde, Jaurès, Millerand, Vaillant, Viviani, Walter.]

Manifeste des députés socialistes au prolétariat, 19 January 1898.

Solidarity of the Left

1. The Young Idealists: Péguy

The student socialists of the Paris Left bank were led by Charles Péguy and the librarian Lucien Herr. Both became committed at an early stage to the ideals of justice, truth, freedom and democracy which the Dreyfusard cause appeared to contain. The pressure of their ideas convinced Millerand and Jaurès that they must not lose this revolutionary opportunity. This letter from Péguy to Millerand was the first declaration of the young socialist intellectuals. Millerand must act or entirely lose their support.

Monsieur
C'est bien simple.
Nous avons assez des discours.
Nous avons trop des combinaisons électorales.
Si vous écrivez encore un seul article dans *l'Eclair* les jeunes socialistes marcheront contre vous jusqu'à la gauche. Nous voulons garder saufs les principes socialistes et non point les situations de ceux qui sont classés socialistes au scrutin d'arrondissement.
Pour mes camarades socialistes

CHARLES PÉGUY

CHARLES PÉGUY to Millerand, 13 January 1898: *Figaro Littéraire*, 4 June 1960.

2. Jaurès

The writings of Jean Jaurès during the Affair can be seen with Zola's as the most sensational Dreyfusard pronouncements. Zola forced intellectuals apart and Jaurès persuaded a large section of socialist opinion to involve itself in the Republic. Following J'accuse, *Jaurès had been prepared to join the Dreyfusard campaign for purely tactical reasons, though he signed the manifesto of neutralism. The fervour of Lucien Herr altered his approach, and he swung round to Dreyfusism out of certainty that the principles of liberty and justice were involved. On 7 July 1898 Cavaignac declared in the chamber that he had certain proof of the guilt of Dreyfus. Jaurès, who had lost his seat in the May elections and was no longer shackled by party discipline, answered with a series of articles in* La Petite République *called* Les Preuves, *fiercely exposing the weakness of the army case against Dreyfus. At the same time he rejected the Manifesto and called on the proletariat to follow him. He distinguishes between laws of injustice in French society, those which buttress capitalism, and laws of progress, those which protect the individual. The latter he declares must be defended by all lovers of liberty. Dreyfus must be seen as an innocent victim, not as a Jew or an officer: he represents all suffering, oppressed people. Socialism is part of the great struggle of humanity. Finally, it is the proletariat which is really menaced by the arbitrary judgment of the army, and its interests can only be protected by defending Dreyfus and shattering the mystery of the in-camera Affair.*

L'INTÉRÊT SOCIALISTE

Ce jour-là, nous aurons le droit de nous dresser, nous socialistes, contre tous les dirigeants qui depuis des années nous combattent au nom des principes de la Révolution française.

'Qu'avez-vous fait, leur crierons-nous, de la déclaration des Droits de l'Homme et de la liberté individuelle? Vous en avez fait mépris; vous avez livré tout cela à l'insolence du pouvoir militaire. Vous êtes les renégats de la Révolution bourgeoise.'

Oh! je sais bien! Et j'entends le sophisme de nos ennemis: 'Quoi! nous dit doucereusement *la Libre Parole*, ce sont des socialistes, des révolutionnaires qui se préoccupent de légalité!'

Je n'ai qu'un mot à répondre. Il y a deux parts dans la légalité capitaliste et bourgeoise. Il y a tout un ensemble de lois destinées à protéger l'iniquité fondamentale de notre société; il y a des lois qui consacrent le privilège de la propriété capitaliste, l'exploitation du salarié par le possédant. Ces lois, nous voulons les rompre, et même par la Révolution, s'il le faut, abolir la légalité capitaliste pour faire surgir un ordre nouveau. Mais à côté de ces lois de privilège et de rapine, faites par une classe et pour elle, il en est d'autres qui résument les pauvres progrès de l'humanité, les modestes garanties qu'elle a peu à peu conquises par le long effort des siècles et la longue suite des Révolutions.

Or parmi ces lois, celle qui ne permet pas de condamner un homme, quel qu'il soit, sans discuter avec lui est la plus essentielle peut-être. Au contraire des nationalistes qui veulent garder de la légalité bourgeoise tout ce qui protège le Capital, et livrer aux généraux tout ce qui protège l'homme, nous, socialistes révolutionnaires, nous voulons, dans la légalité d'aujourd'hui, abolir la portion capitaliste et sauver la portion humaine. Nous défendons les garanties légales contre les juges galonnés qui les brisent, comme nous défendrions au besoin la légalité républicaine contre des généraux de coup d'état.

Oh! je sais bien encore et ici ce sont des amis qui parlent: 'Il ne s'agit pas, disent-ils, d'un prolétaire; laissons les bourgeois s'occuper des bourgeois.' Et l'un d'eux ajoutait cette phrase qui, je l'avoue, m'a peiné: 'S'il s'agissait d'un ouvrier, il y a longtemps qu'on ne s'en occuperait plus.'

Je pourrais répondre que si Dreyfus a été illégalement condamné et si, en effet, comme je le démontrerai bientôt, il est innocent, il n'est plus ni un officier ni un bourgeois: il est dépouillé, par l'excès même du malheur, de tout caractère de classe; il n'est plus que l'humanité elle-même, au plus haut degré de misère et de désespoir qui se puisse imaginer.

Si on l'a condamné contre toute loi, si on l'a condamné à faux, quelle dérision de le compter encore parmi les privilégiés! Non: il n'est plus de cette armée qui, par une erreur criminelle, l'a dégradé. Il n'est plus de ces classes dirigeantes qui par poltronnerie d'ambition hésitent à rétablir pour lui la légalité et la vérité. Il est seulement un exemplaire de l'humaine souffrance en ce qu'elle a de plus poignant. Il est le témoin vivant du mensonge militaire, de la lâcheté politique, des crimes de l'autorité.

Certes, nous pouvons, sans contredire nos principes et sans manquer à la lutte des classes, écouter le cri de notre pitié; nous pouvons dans le combat révolutionnaire garder des entrailles humaines; nous ne sommes pas tenus, pour rester dans le socialisme, de nous enfuir hors de l'humanité.

Et Dreyfus lui-même, condamné à faux et criminellement par la société que nous combattons, devient, quelles qu'aient été ses origines, et quel que doive être son destin, une protestation aiguë contre l'ordre social. Par la faute de la société qui s'obstine contre lui à la violence, au mensonge et au crime, il devient un élément de Révolution.

Voilà ce que je pourrais répondre; mais j'ajoute que les socialistes qui veulent fouiller jusqu'au fond les secrets de honte et de crime contenus dans cette affaire, s'ils ne s'occupent pas *d'un ouvrier*, s'occupent *de toute la classe ouvrière*.

Qui donc est le plus menacé aujourd'hui par l'arbitraire des généraux, par la violence toujours glorifiée des répressions militaires? Qui? Le prolétariat. Il a donc un intérêt de premier ordre à châtier et à décourager les illégalités et les violences des conseils de guerre avant qu'elles deviennent une sorte d'habitude acceptée de tous. Il a un intérêt de premier ordre à précipiter le discrédit moral et la chute de cette haute armée réactionnaire qui est prête à le foudroyer demain.

Puisque, cette fois, c'est à un fils de la bourgeoisie que la haute armée, égarée par des luttes de clan, a appliqué son système d'arbitraire et de mensonge, la société bourgeoise est plus profondément remuée et ébranlée, et nous devons profiter de cet ébranlement pour diminuer la force morale et la puissance d'agression de ces Etats-Majors rétrogrades qui sont une menace directe pour le prolétariat.

Ce n'est donc pas servir seulement l'humanité, c'est servir directement la classe ouvrière que de protester, comme nous le faisons, contre l'illégalité, maintenant démontrée, du procès Dreyfus et contre la monstrueuse prétention d'Alphonse Humbert de sceller à jamais ce crime militaire dans l'impénétrabilité du huis clos.

J. JAURÈS: *Les Preuves*, La Petite République, 1898, pp. 11–14.

3. A Dreyfusard Catechism

Written by a supporter of Jaurès, this is a fascinating attempt to make the word 'intellectual' acceptable to the socialist rank and file. The Syndicate, of which so much was made, is turned here into an association of socialists and intellectuals who are men acting independently, and inspired by great ideals. The working man can easily be an intellectual if Brunetière can be a stupid ass. (For Brunetière's article on the army see Sources, p. 46, no. 2.)

Qui êtes-vous?
Enfant de France aimant sa patrie.
Que voulez-vous?
Être du Syndicat.
Qu'entendez-vous par là?
M'associer aux hommes qui sacrifient leur bien-être, leur tranquillité, leurs relations, leur réputation, leur liberté pour le triomphe d'une idée de justice. En un mot, je veux être parmi les intellectuels tels que Bernard Lazare, Zola, Duclaux, Yves Guyot, Jaurès, et autres.
Qu'est-ce qu'un intellectuel?
C'est un homme dont le cerveau refuse de fonctionner *par ordre* et dont les plus petites actions s'inspirent des plus grands principes.
Un ouvrier peut donc être aussi un intellectuel?
Du moment qu'un membre de l'Institut comme Brunetière peut être un âne-vel, rien ne s'oppose à ce qu'un ouvrier soit intellectuel.

J. LEMAZURIER: *Catéchisme Dreyfusard*, Stock, 1898.

4. Anarchists: Faure

Sébastien Faure, one of the most prominent anarchists, became a more convinced Dreyfusard than many socialists. As early as 15 December 1897 he held a meeting which declared for revision, and he and Louise Michel, another anarchist, both backed the Ligue des Droits de l'Homme. Such positive action would seem inconsistent with anarchist ideology, and Faure defends himself against this criticism in this pamphlet. Anarchists, he says, must not remain on the outside, but take part for their own interests and to warn the public against all forms of injustice. It is only human to help a suffering individual. We are members of the Syndicate of revolution against all the forces of oppression.

... ne pas rester totalement étrangers au mouvement, ne pas entrer comme affiliés dans la conspiration, mais se mêler à l'agitation et profiter d'un cas particulier et des batailles qu'il suscite, pour aborder le développement des thèses générales qui nous sont chères, mettre le public en garde contre les funestes emballements et dire ce que nous pensons notamment de la justice militaire ou civile, de l'armée, des chefs, du patriotisme, des religions, de l'antisémitisme, de la presse, de l'opinion publique...

... Quand un homme est tombé, quand il souffre, quand il se meurt, on ne lui demande ni sa nationalité, ni ses opinions politiques, ni sa foi, ni ses antécédants. On lui vient en aide, on l'arrache au danger, on le dispute à la mort. C'est spontané, c'est bon, c'est humain.

... Du Syndicat? Oui nous en sommes. Il s'agit seulement de savoir duquel. Il y en a deux qui embrassent le monde et pour lesquels il n'y a ni patrie, ni religion, ni race: le syndicat de la richesse et celui de la pauvreté, la Fédération des Maîtres et celle des Révoltés.

L'heure est venue d'opter, il faut se décider. Notre choix, à nous, est fait. Nous sommes du syndicat de la révolte contre l'oppression civile et militaire, contre la guerre et l'armée, contre la religion et les prêtres, contre le capital et l'exploitation, contre l'État et les propriétaires, contre toutes les institutions et croyances qui mutilent l'individu, stérilisent l'effort et endolorissent la vie.

SÉBASTIEN FAURE: *Les Anarchistes et l'Affaire Dreyfus*, Lafont, 1898, pp. 7, 12, 32.

Monarchist Revivalism

1. The Ideology: Maurras

In November 1897 Charles Maurras quite suddenly became convinced that a monarchy was the only possible régime for France. It alone, he believed, could reunite the broken fragments of French life and give the nation authority, purpose and power. He scorned parliamentary democracy for its party system and its political compromises. He wanted a France that was one; a nation which was a measurable entity. In this ideal lay the tyranny of his thought and his threat to the Republic. After his passionate defence of Colonel Henry (see Sources, p. 41, no. 2), his anti-Dreyfusism became more openly anti-republican, and in 1899 he began an enquiry into the amount of monarchist feeling in France. By choosing his samples carefully he built up a massive volume of monarchist ideas: a handbook for his movement Action Française over the next forty-five years. André Buffet, interviewed in this extract, had been exiled for his part in Déroulède's attempted coup d'état at President Faure's funeral. He was a dedicated royalist working for the Bourbon Duke of Orleans. The dialogue is heavily stylised and reads like a parody. But the seriousness of both Maurras and Buffet should not be doubted.

The Monarchy, Buffet begins, can resolve all problems. Maurras agrees and tells Buffet of the sad state of France. In the slang of a young nationalist he describes France as murderous. Buffet is not surprised and adds that France will probably accept any brutal government in its present state. He hopes that it won't be deluded into accepting the mere semblance of a strong government. France needs a definite solution—Maurras prompts 'A monarchy?' and Buffet describes the true strength of monarchic force. A republic, he believes, is arbitrary, whereas a monarch has to be flexible and in touch with public needs, since his life depends on it. In the present circumstances a monarchy in France would have to be ruthless. The insults to which France is being subjected must be met forcibly, as the royalist prince, the Duke of Orleans, has said. The monarchy will do all that is necessary.

— Parlez, dit-il, je répondrai à toutes vos interrogations. Il n'y a pas une seule question politique que la Monarchie ne doive envisager.

'Elle peut les résoudre toutes.'

Je répondis que telle était ma conviction, en effet, et, comme André Buffet me pressait de questions nouvelles, sur l'état de l'opinion à Paris et en province:

— Cette opinion, lui dis-je, n'a pas changé ... La France voudrait maintenant qu'on fût audacieux pour elle et que ses ennemis fussent défiés en son nom ...

M. André Buffet me marquait en silence son assentiment. Je me rappelai un exemple.

— Le jour même de mon départ pour Bruxelles, ajoutai-je, un jeune nationaliste des faubourgs me donnait, dans un langage brutal, la formule abrégée de tous les vœux de la nation:

— La France? me dit-il, la France? Elle n'est pas républicaine, ni bonapartiste, ni royaliste non plus.

'Voulez-vous le savoir? — La France, elle est poignarde!'

En parfait parisien, M. André Buffet n'est pas ignorant de l'argot. Et l'horrible mot de *poignarde* ne l'a pas fait sourciller.

Il répète même:

— Poignarde, c'est cela peut-être ...

'Je crois, en effet, que la France affolée, énervée, désorientée, sera malheureusement tentée de se déclarer pour le premier gouvernement *à poigne* qui lui semblera patriote, c'est-à-dire antijuif, c'est-à-dire opposé au parti de Dreyfus. La France, tête et cœur, peuple et élite, aspire à être gouvernée. Elle veut un régime fort.

'Mais, voyez-vous, le contraire de la vraie force, c'est parfois, c'est souvent l'apparence de la force. Dieu veuille que la France ne se laisse pas tromper par cette apparence! L'expérience serait mortelle.

'Du reste, j'ai la conviction que l'expérience ne sera pas faite. L'histoire de ces dernières années le prouve. La France est un malade qui a peur du chirurgien: aussi chacun vient-il lui parler d'une foule de charlatans, d'empiriques et de drogueurs. Elle écoute avec complaisance tout ce qu'on lui en dit, mais attend sans se décider. Pourtant le mal s'aggrave, la douleur presse, la fin menace: il faut bien se résoudre à l'intervention. Je souhaite que la France s'y résolve à temps.'

M. Buffet se tut.

— Alors, dis-je, la Monarchie sera donc ce régime fort *qu'il faut* à la France?

— Elle seule le serait nécessairement, me répond-il.

'Ce qui est admirable dans la Monarchie, c'est la souplesse. C'est la variété de sa force.

'Parlementaire ou plébiscitaire, une République dépend de l'esprit et du cœur de ses républicains. Mais un souverain héréditaire est trop directement intéressé au bien public pour gouverner uniquement d'après son humeur ou d'après un système. Il est le cerveau, le système nerveux central de la nation. Il frémit du danger commun, il aspire à la commune prospérité. Sa nature profonde, sa fonction nécessaire et naturelle ou, si vous préférez user du langage des géomètres, sa *position* l'obligent à se régler sur les nécessités du salut public. Il peut se tromper, sans doute, dans la vue de ces nécessités, mais il est forcé de les chercher et, l'erreur à peine aperçue, il est induit *par son intérêt* à la corriger . . .'

— Il n'y a pas d'erreur possible en ce moment, interrompis-je.

— Non, il n'y en a pas. Les circonstances actuelles doivent rendre la monarchie 'poignarde', comme dit votre ami.

'Disons, si vous voulez, autoritaire.

'Rien de plus facile à la Monarchie. Ne dépendant aucunement de l'élection et n'étant pas contrainte à flatter l'opinion par des excès inutiles, la Monarchie aura tout ensemble la force de sévir comme il le faudra, et la force, plus rare encore, de modérer une trop juste répression.

'On opprime l'armée. On trahit la nation. Vous connaissez, par ses discours et par ses lettres, Monsieur le duc d'Orléans. Le Prince est un soldat. Il ne sépare point les deux termes, peuple et armée. Souvenez-vous de sa parole: *Je ne vengerai que les injures faites à la Patrie.* Mais ces injures-ci, soyez-en convaincu, il les vengera.

'Voulez-vous l'exacte mesure d'une répression monarchique?

'*Elle fera le nécessaire. Rien que le nécessaire. Mais tout le nécessaire.*'

C. MAURRAS: *Enquête sur la Monarchie* (1st edn. 1900), Bibliothèque des œuvres politiques, Versailles, 1928, pp. 38–40.

2. Scepticism: Barrès

Barrès and Maurras had much in common, especially a hostility towards the ruling republicans and a devotion to the traditions of old France. But Barrès was no monarchist: he was too realistic to entertain the illusions of Maurras. Despite his antagonism to Dreyfusards, like Jaurès and Clemenceau, he recognised that such men and their ideas were an inevitable part of modern France. At times he called them aliens, but he made no attempt, like Maurras, to construct a theoretical nation without them. His reply to Maurras was therefore sceptical of the monarchist's ideology. On practical grounds alone, he writes, it is impossible: there is no obvious monarch, there is no real aristocracy left, since the submission of the noble estate at the time of the Revolution (4 August 1789), and the sentiments of the people are republican. Why not improve the régime which the majority accepts, by reforms bringing authority to the top and decentralisation elsewhere?

Et non seulement elle vous manque, cette famille que possèdent l'Allemagne, la Russie et à laquelle ces pays se rallient par une adhésion instinctive, en quelque sorte pieuse, mais plus encore vous manquez d'une aristocratie (corps indispensable, n'est-ce pas? à votre monarchie traditionnelle).... Ces nobles qui, dans la Nuit du 4 août, ont presque comiquement annulé leurs pouvoirs, que reste-t-il d'eux? Voyez: ils ne savent même point se purger des rastaquouères qui leur donnent peu à peu les plus ignobles couleurs.

Je ne date pas d'un siècle l'histoire de France, mais je ne puis non plus méconnaître ses périodes les plus récentes. Elles ont disposé nos concitoyens de telle sorte qu'ils réservent pour le principe républicain ces puissances de sentiment que d'autres nations accordent au principe d'hérédité et sans lesquelles un gouvernement ne peut subsister.

Ne pouvant faire que ce qui vous paraît raisonnable soit accepté de tous, pourquoi ne tâchez-vous pas que ce que la majorité accepte devienne raisonnable? Au sommet de l'Etat l'autorité, sur le sol et dans les groupes, la décentralisation, voilà des réformes que permet le système républicain et qui assureraient le développement des forces françaises aujourd'hui gravement anémiées.

Affectueusement votre dévoué,

MAURICE BARRÈS

In C. Maurras, *Enquête sur la Monarchie*, p. 135.

Part Three
THE AFFAIR IN HISTORY

By the time the Affair fell away from the headlines in the winter of 1899 the answers given to the question 'What was really at issue?' had been numerous and diffuse. The Socialist Manifesto saw the Affair as a fratricidal struggle among the bourgeoisie, Drumont as the nemesis of the Jews, Reinach as the subversion of the Jesuits, Clemenceau as the fight for individual rights and *La Croix* as the aggression of free-thinkers. The examples could be sustained to introduce almost all conceivable explanations. In the heat of the Affair the difficulty of objective analysis was extreme. Even when the bellows of journalism were removed the fire continued to burn those who approached it. In the period between 1899 and the First War the contestants made their polemics into theses: the variety of explanations given during the Affair were perpetuated in interpretative writings which became history or fiction according to one's standpoint.

The History of the Affair which Reinach produced has a width and reliability of detail which surpassed all other attempts in this first period, but every time he postulates a general interpretation he betrays his anticlerical Dreyfusism of which he was proud and conscious.[1] A rival version came from two anti-Dreyfusards, Delebecque and Larpent, writing under the name Henri Dutrait-Crozon, whose *Précis de l'Affaire Dreyfus* in 1909 was a subtle mosaic of historical narration, pure invention and antisemitism. Beginning their chapter on Picquart and Esterhazy they wrote:

> The Jews wanted the minister of war to initiate revision. They charged Picquart to persuade his chiefs to substitute Esterhazy for Dreyfus. But this substitution was only possible if Esterhazy had identical writing to that of the 'bordereau'.... The collaboration of Esterhazy with the Jews was thus indispensable for the success of their plan. Esterhazy therefore began to model his writing on that of the 'bordereau'... this rôle was not as dangerous for him as it might appear. His manoeuvres to pose as the author of Dreyfus's crime would expose him to a court martial. But he could almost

[1] See Sources, p. 83, no. 3.

certainly count on an acquittal since Dreyfus had already been unanimously condemned.... Once this acquittal was achieved, it was perfectly safe for Esterhazy to continue his agitation in favour of Dreyfus, even to declaring that he had himself written the 'bordereau'. In this way he gave double service to the Jews. They could accuse the General Staff firstly of condemning Dreyfus when they knew he was innocent and secondly of acquitting Esterhazy when they knew he was guilty.[1]

Of all the intriguing inventions in the historiography of the Affair this was one of the most influential. It made the Affair into a giant conspiracy against the army and the General Staff, and even more into a deliberate sabotage of national unity. It was this charge that Charles Maurras reiterated to the end of his polemical life. In 1931 he repeated Dutrait-Crozon's version and drew his own particular moral: the weakening of France by the Affair cost her the lives of her best sons in the carnage of 1914-18. France divided became France unprepared, and France unprepared was slaughtered in the trenches of the long campaigns.[2] What Dutrait-Crozon did not know and Maurras deliberately forgot was that the Affair, by rallying many socialists to the Republic, gave a precedent for the union of all parties at the outbreak of war in 1914. This is not to suggest that the republican solidarity of 1899 was identical with the *Union Sacrée* of 1914, but there are enough similarities to challenge the Maurrasian school of thought.

Another critic of the standard Dreyfusism embodied in Reinach's History was Georges Sorel, the philosopher of violence and exponent of revolutionary syndicalism. A man of intellect but an anti-intellectual, he stood back from the Affair and exposed it to his biting scorn. The title he used was *La Révolution Dreyfusienne* (1909), but in any comparison with the great Revolution the Affair emerges badly. Although it brought results which he endorsed, especially the anticlerical legislation of Waldeck-Rousseau and Combes, he claims it was fought by mediocre men in their own interests. The Dreyfusards, he states, can be clearly seen; they have reaped all the social and political honour; no myths of greatness will ever surround them; they are men who have won and taken the fruits of victory; they have had no glorious death like the revolutionaries in 1793. In the chapter 'Ostensible and Real Motives' he lampoons the hypocrisy and pomp of the

---

[1] H. Dutrait-Crozon: *Précis de l'Affaire Dreyfus*, 1909, p. 55.
[2] See Sources, p. 129, no. 3.

'heroes', especially the literary ones, from whom he selects Zola for particular sarcasm.

> At the beginning of Zola's trial the president of the court observed that Zola ought to have conformed to article 52 of the law on the press. Zola replied with magnificent stupidity, 'I do not know the law and I do not wish to know it.' At the fifth session Zola felt the need to tell the jury what a distance there was between himself and his adversaries. '... I leave to posterity the name of General de Pellieux and that of Emile Zola. It will chose.' I'm afraid it is rather unfortunate for Zola's memory that the two are fairly equal.[1]

Sorel at this period was a regular contributor to the *Cahiers de la Quinzaine*, a periodic publication of literature and comment inspired and run by Charles Péguy, and it was in this series that two Dreyfusard idealists wrote their reflections and gave their interpretation of the Affair. Daniel Halévy, essayist, critic and historian of the early Third Republic, called his memoirs *Apologie pour notre passé* (1910) and said that what really moved the young Dreyfusards was the fact of an innocent condemned, and to this sentiment they mixed the Revolutionary ideals of justice and rational humanitarianism. But, he added:

> ... although Dreyfus was not absent from our thoughts when we began our campaign he was a long way away, far away on that small island where his wretched body and soul were being tortured. Another victim claimed our closer attention. France, poisoned with fear and hatred by a small group of men, was losing its honour: innocent France was being murdered.

But Halévy did not intend to fight the old battles over again and as he described the Dreyfusard action, often with nostalgic and evocative phrases, a pacific and conciliatory note crept into his writing. In the next to last paragraph he concludes:

> The victim is vindicated: the guilty punished. It is all over, and so much the better. We shall keep our memories which bring us honour and which will never disgrace us: we shall even honour the crisis, which was brutal but not unhealthy, and which will make us continue our efforts, but we will NOT BOAST OF BEING VICTORIOUS, for the issue was confused.[2]

Charles Péguy could not agree. The caution of his friend alarmed him. For Péguy there was no confusion. In *Notre Jeunesse* (1910) he replied to Halévy with a panegyric on the heroes of the Affair and a

[1] For reference and a further extract see Sources, p. 24, no. 4.
[2] Daniel Halévy: *Apologie pour notre passé*, 1910, pp. 38 and 115.

brilliant generalisation on the degeneration of movements from a mystique of hopes and ideals to the politics of ambition and interest: 'Tout commence en mystique et finit en politique.' The clarity of this perception is striking. It allowed him to divide those whose ideals remained untrammelled by politics from those who, as Sorel had stated, reaped the political fruits of victory. He himself was proud to be among the consistent idealists and to proclaim his undiluted faith in the mystique of the early Dreyfusards. His interpretation of the Affair is an alluring one. His analysis is dynamic: those who had been right during the crisis could become wrong in victory. There is no static identification of Dreyfusards with virtue and anti-Dreyfusards with vice.[1] But his idealism has not been unchallenged. In 1931 the socialist Alexander Zévaès dismissed it as the intoxication of a young man who was unable to see the realities of the situation. But Zévaès had his own beliefs to justify, especially his faith in the heroic rôle of socialism in the making of modern France, and such a criterion is no less subjective as a guide to the Dreyfus Affair than the poetic vision of Péguy.[2]

Before we leave the prewar period mention must be made of the Affair in literature. Zola, Anatole France, Marcel Proust and Roger Martin du Gard were all Dreyfusards and all incorporated the course and passions of the Affair into their novels. Zola's *Vérité* (1903 posthumous), the third of his four new but unfinished gospels; Maternity, Work, Truth and Justice, was inspired by the Affair, though the characters bear only a superficial resemblance to the original participants: it is hard to decide whether his hero is Bernard Lazare or Picquart. No such obscurity surrounds the criminals of the novel who are openly the clericals, portrayed with vehemence but little concern for realism: the naturalism of Zola's earlier novels has been largely superseded by a system of belief and pungent invective. Anatole France had started as a severe critic of Zola's literature, but during the Affair the cause of Dreyfusism brought them together. The cynic became a convinced apostle of progress, justice and reason and his funeral oration for Zola in 1902 is of rich optimistic eloquence.[3] The Affair was treated with just as much enthusiasm in *M. Bergeret à Paris* (1901), in which the anti-Dreyfusards are mercilessly satirised and drawn as the evil promoters of error and injustice. This was the new ebullient Anatole France, but by 1908 and his novel *L'Ile des*

[1] See Sources, p. 123, no. 1.   [2] See Sources, p. 125, no. 2.
[3] See Sources, p. 23, no. 3.

Pingouins he had returned to cynicism. There is little in common between his allegory of Dreyfusism and his own earlier faith in the Dreyfusard cause, and the anti-Dreyfusards are treated with tired mockery.[1] Anatole France finally rallied to an individual type of communism, though politics became less and less important to him.

Marcel Proust, unlike Anatole France and Zola, did not write polemically about the Affair, but used it as a touchstone by which to measure his characters. He stressed the subjectivity with which most of them approached it, and in particular, since he was conscious of his Jewish origins, he was fascinated by the impact of the racial tensions on the society of his novels. He makes it clear that the moment when the salons divided over the Affair was when Zola and Clemenceau launched their full campaign in *L'Aurore*. At once the more aristocratic salons of the Boulevard Saint Germain became anti-Dreyfusard. But in Proust's world the crosscurrents of fashion assured that these salons were not totally closed to the supporters of Dreyfus: in particular, Mme Verdurin, although a Dreyfusard, found the doors of society opened by her friendship with the Russian musicians who were in vogue at the time. With Picquart balanced by Stravinsky and Labori by Nijinski, Dreyfusism remained in social circulation.[2] The Affair was not only excellent material for Proust's novels, it also played an important part in his own evolution, pulling him away from his aristocratic contacts and from the nationalists and antisemites in high society whose ideas he found bigoted and stupid. His attitude was one of pessimism, and in this he drew close to the disenchanted phase of Anatole France. But Proust did not simplify the Affair: he understood and portrayed its complexities.

Jean Barois, by Roger Martin du Gard, has already been mentioned. Written in 1913, it recaptured the period of ideological division with great clarity. Although the actions of his characters have a certain predictability and large elements of the history of the Affair are inserted en bloc, his situations are never too contrived nor his characters too artificial. His evocation of Dreyfusard enthusiasm is colourful and romantic:[3] it expresses some of the poetry and mystique which Péguy wished to preserve.

Like the prewar histories and interpretations of the Affair, these

---

[1] See Sources, p. 80, no. 5.
[2] Cécile Delhorbe: *L'Affaire Dreyfus et les Ecrivains français*, 1932, p. 250: a book of immense value, to which I am considerably indebted.
[3] See Sources, p. 20, no. 2.

Cassation

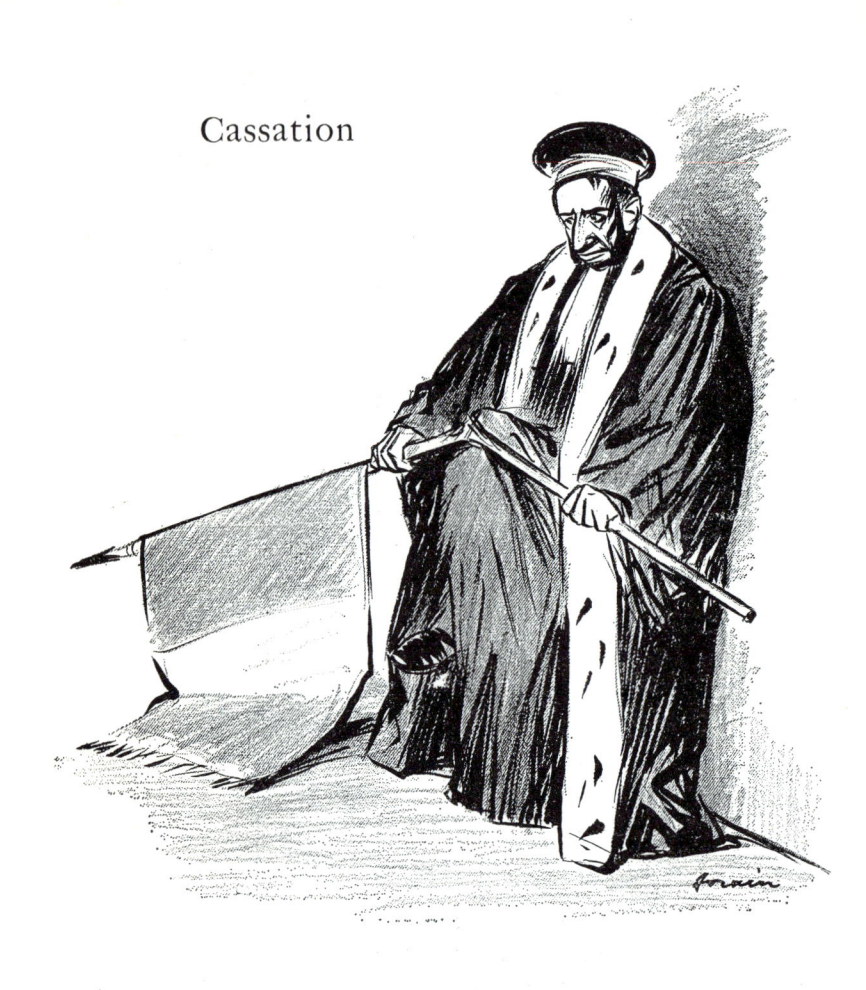

From the Anti-Dreyfusard *Le Psst!*, 9 April 1898

novels were based on personal memory. Between 1929 and 1936, against the background of conflict between democracy and fascism, new accounts were written by men who had not lived through the Affair but who found its history both intriguing and relevant. New perspectives were gained by the publication of documents, and the death of Alfred Dreyfus in 1935 provided a fresh stimulus to interpretation. Documents of the Affair had been published at various intervals, notably in the collection by Louis Leblois, the old Dreyfusard lawyer,[1] but one vital source of evidence had remained silent. Colonel Schwartzkoppen, whom Zola had said would alone give the full truth, died in 1917 without a public statement, and his widow continued his reticence. But in 1930 she was provoked to publish her husband's notebooks (*Carnets*), and the publishers proudly subtitled them *La vérité sur Dreyfus*.[2] Esterhazy's treasonous dealings with the German Military Attaché were clearly revealed. These new revelations were quickly assimilated by historians, and for the first time unimpassioned accounts of the Affair began to be written. Among these the *Historique de l'Affaire Dreyfus*, by Armand Charpentier, stands out as calmly objective, and the history by Charensol was almost impartial, though he was eager to see the republican mystique of the Dreyfusards reintroduced in the France of the 1930s.[3]

Besides these, and the history by Zévaès already discussed, Schwartzkoppen's *Carnets* stimulated also a piece of sheer fantasy. In 1934 Henri Mazel, under the impressive title *Histoire et psychologie de l'Affaire Dreyfus*, ascribed the whole plot to Schwartzkoppen himself, who, he claimed, forged the 'bordereau' in the belligerent spirit of the Kaiser, who was anti-French, and thus initiated a great crisis in France which weakened the morale and unity of the country. The author was serious.

In July 1935 the death of Dreyfus, a quietly retired old man who had served with honour in the 1914–18 War, occasioned not only a crop of variously slanted obituaries but also Léon Blum's *Souvenirs sur l'Affaire* (1935), which are immensely readable and full of perception. Léon Blum, the socialist leader of the 1930s, was a politician scarcely less controversial than Jaurès during the Affair. Central as he was to the Popular Front alignment against antirepublican nationalists and fascists, it is not surprising that he talks of the Affair as concluded in its

---

[1] Louis Leblois: *L'Affaire Dreyfus. Les principaux faits et les principaux documents*, 1929.
[2] See Sources, p. 120, no. 1.   [3] See Sources, p. 128, no. 2.

detective aspect, but undecided as an ideological controversy. But he also has a more questionable interpretation to offer. At the end of his memoirs he concludes that the Affair, like a war, was an interruption of normality; after it life returned to pre-existing patterns: the storm was over and calm returned.[1] As a means of emphasising the passionate outburst of opinions which the Affair provoked, this conclusion is easily justified, but behind it there is a philosophy of modern France, a plain broken by mountains, which is controversial. One might suggest that the Affair was normality expressed in an extreme manner rather than the interjection of an abnormal situation. But this would be only to adapt his interpretation, not to reject it.

Since the 1930s, publications on the Affair have become more academic. This may seem surprising, since the period of Vichy and the Resistance displayed many of the characteristics of the Affair and might have led to a new wave of retrospection and interpretation. But the peculiar nature and intensity of the internal conflict of these years encouraged concentration on the issue in hand. There was little time or inclination to explore historical parallels.

In recent years research has centred more on the questions left unanswered by the various trials and enquiries between 1894 and 1906 than on the ideological conflict, although the fiftieth anniversary of *J'accuse* was celebrated by a special account of Zola's involvement in the Affair.[2] But controversies remain. Since Maurice Paléologue, a foreign office official, published in 1955 his secret diary of the Affair, several works, notably that of Marcel Thomas, *L'Affaire sans Dreyfus*, have been devoted to clearing the mists which have surrounded Esterhazy's relations with the General Staff. There is considerable argument over which officers were as culpable of deceit as Colonel Henry, a problem which lies beyond this book. The concentration here has been on Blum's 'autre Affaire', the conflict of opinion.

In summary, the historiography of the Affair has tended to perpetuate the original conflicts, discussing not only who was guilty but also the wider problem of what the Affair was really about. Memoirs, like those of Péguy, Halévy, Maurras and Blum, have been particularly valuable for re-creating the atmosphere of the Affair: even François Mauriac's introduction to a recent edition of Dreyfus's diary and letters achieves this effect, even though he was only nine at the time. When he tells us that his chamber pot was called Zola a recog-

[1] See Sources, p. 122, no. 2.
[2] A. Zévaès: *Le Cinquantenaire de J'accuse*, 1948.

nisable picture of a provincial Catholic family quickly comes to mind.[1] But the memoirs are limited and the Affair badly needs its social historian. One needs to know how deeply the conflicts penetrated into the provinces: how, for example, the provincial meetings of the Ligue des Droits de l'Homme were received. One also wants to know where the finances for the various papers came from, and how far the economic world was involved in other aspects of the Affair, like the avoidance of revision. It has frequently been suggested that Méline's government was interested less in avoiding revision than in keeping out a Radical government which was determined to introduce income tax. And, enquiring further, why was violence avoided? There were certainly many of the prerequisites for violence: enflamed passions, organised gangs, demagogic leaders and a weak political situation, but civil war was averted. Why had Paris since the Commune of 1871 lost its revolutionary tradition?

More widely, one looks for periods of conflict which can usefully be compared to the Affair. The peculiarity of its tensions means that its closest parallels lie in the other crises in modern French history to which frequent allusion has been made. Beyond these there is a close similarity in the Calas case in eighteenth-century France, which Bruno Weil used as the preface to his book on Dreyfus in 1930.[2] Certainly the hostility which Voltaire met in Catholic circles and the central fact of an act of injustice upheld by prejudice would make the comparison particularly acceptable to anticlerical interpreters of the Affair. For those who see the racial question as dominant there are similarities in the present South African situation, where the coloured races are said to work in conjunction with subversive left-wing politics and the white population to have the vested backing of certain churches. However true these accusations may be, it is apparent that the two sides have their own particular view of the future of South Africa; views which, like those of Drumont and Bernard Lazare, or Maurras and Zola, it seems impossible to reconcile.

In a sense any war, civil war or revolution is a catalyst for tensions in society. The personal rule of King Charles I in the seventeenth century brought to a head the tensions between parliament and the court, lawyers and the king's advisers, Puritanism and Anglicanism, and between an emerging capitalism and an obsolete economic orthodoxy. In the twentieth century the murder of the Archduke

---

[1] A. Dreyfus: *Cinq années de ma vie*. Preface by François Mauriac, 1962.
[2] See Sources, p. 127, no. 1.

Ferdinand at Sarajevo in 1914 achieved the same catalytic effect for the tensions in Europe. Just as one can analyse the Affair in terms of pre-existing social antagonisms and ideological conflicts, so one can look for the origins of the English Civil War and the First World War in the mounting tensions which preceded them. This approach does not lessen the importance of the catalysing factor: it attempts to improve its perspective. Whether examining the conviction of Dreyfus, the execution of Jean Calas, the murder of Thomas à Becket or the assassination of Franz Ferdinand, the historian will want more than a detective story. He will want to know why these events divided opinion, and to answer this question he will probe in depth and explore in width. The Dreyfus Affair stems from the France of 1894, it evokes the France of the Revolution and foreshadows the France of Vichy and the Resistance. But its affinities are not confined to France.

SOURCES

Truth of the Affair?

1. The Traitor: Schwartzkoppen's Carnets

The German Military Attaché, Colonel Schwartzkoppen, refused to say a word in public throughout the Affair. Many revisionists tried to provoke some kind of statement from him, but he would not be drawn. To say he had been in relation with any French traitor would have been to compromise himself and Germany. He died in 1917. In 1930 fragments of one of his letters at the time of the Affair were published by Bruno Weil in Germany, and they appeared to endanger Schwartzkoppen's reputation. His widow decided that his full notebooks should be published to clear his name. They were at once translated into French with the sub-title 'The Truth about Dreyfus'. Despite this assertion, not everyone was convinced. A small number of persistent anti-Dreyfusards, including Charles Maurras, pointed out that the Carnets were an account written in 1903, not in 1894. This lapse in time, they suggested, would have allowed him to be influenced by the early volumes of Reinach's history. Nor, they said, could Schwartzkoppen say definitely who wrote the 'bordereau', since he had never received it. But despite these criticisms, his account of his relations with Esterhazy have been generally accepted. The real traitor is here presented. A Frenchman offers his treason to save his family from ruin: all other ways of making money had failed. He claimed to know the military situation at first hand and produced a sample of secret documents. Schwartzkoppen is surprised and shocked and sends him away, but the man returns. He introduces himself as Count Esterhazy.

Le 20 juillet 1894, entre 3 et 4 heures de l'après-midi, un Français se présenta chez moi, au bureau militaire de l'ambassade d'Allemagne à Paris . . .

. . . A ma question sur l'objet de sa visite, il se présenta à moi comme un officier d'Etat-major français en service actif, contraint par la nécessité de faire une démarche qui le rendrait méprisable à mes yeux, mais à laquelle il avait bien réfléchi et qu'il était forcé de faire pour sauver sa femme et ses enfants de la misère et de la ruine certaine. Des circonstances défavorables, des spéculations malheureuses, la maladie de sa femme l'avaient placé dans une situation économique difficile et, pour pouvoir conserver à sa famille une petite propriété qu'il possédait près de Châlons, il lui fallait se procurer de l'argent à tout prix. Tous ses efforts pour le faire d'une manière honnête et légale avaient échoué; il ne lui restait donc qu'une seule issue, c'était d'offrir ses services à l'Etat-major allemand, dans l'espoir que de cette façon, il se trouverait rapidement en état de faire face à ses multiples obligations. Il y avait mûrement réfléchi, et c'était la seule voie qui lui restât encore ouverte; s'il échouait, il serait obligé de se loger une balle dans la tête. Mais la pensée de sa femme malade et de ses enfants l'avaient jusque là empêché de prendre ce parti extrême, quoiqu'il se rendit fort bien compte que c'était là ce qu'il avait de mieux à faire. Il était parfaitement en état de rendre des services importants, car il avait passé beaucoup de temps en Algérie et était tout à fait au courant des conditions militaires de ce pays; il avait aussi passé pas mal de temps à la frontière italienne et connaissait à fond l'organisation de la défense de la frontière; pendant les années 1881 et 1882, il avait travaillé au Bureau des Renseignements du ministère de la Guerre.

. . . Comme preuve qu'il était déjà en possession de renseignements importants, il tira de la poche intérieure de son veston un écrit qu'il me présenta en me demandant de le lire.

J'étais extrêmement surpris et indigné de cette offre! Un officier d'Etat-major français en activité de service qui ne rougit pas de devenir un traître à sa patrie, et qui, sans ambages, demande à un membre de sa profession, à un camarade, de lui servir d'intermédiaire!

Je lui répondis, en lui rendant son écrit sans le lire, que ce n'était nullement mon rôle d'aider un officier à s'écarter de la voie du devoir et de l'honneur.

... Le 27 juillet, celui-ci revint à mon bureau, sans m'avoir prévenu, et se présenta désormais comme le commandant comte Walsin-Esterhazy, chef de bataillon au 74e régiment d'infanterie à Rouen.

Les Carnets de Schwartzkoppen: La vérité sur Dreyfus, Editions Rieder, 1930, pp. 5–10.

2. The Two Affairs: Léon Blum

Léon Blum can be placed among the young socialists and idealists who were in the forefront of the Dreyfusard cause and for whom 'all was clear, luminous, self-evident' as he himself has said. By 1935 he was the leader of the Socialist party in France, and when Dreyfus died in that year Blum published his Memoirs of the Affair. They are a sensitive evocation of the passions and beliefs of the Dreyfusards and his portraits of the leading revisionists are excellent. In this extract he separates the Affair into two: the Affair specifically about Dreyfus—was he guilty or innocent?—and the Affair which was the division of France into conflicting ideologies. The former, he is convinced, has ended: no thinking man still believes Dreyfus to be guilty. The latter, however, had no result: no side, he suggests, really triumphed. In fact, despite the passions of the Affair, France soon returned to normal as if nothing had happened. This statement is Blum's most controversial contribution to the historiography of the Affair.

'L'Affaire' que je viens d'évoquer ainsi, c'est celle qui a été gagnée, franchement et complètement gagnée, puisque Dreyfus a pu servir pendant la guerre avec ses galons d'officier, puisqu'il vient de mourir vieux et tranquille entre les siens, puisqu'il n'existe plus au monde, dans aucun pays, un seul être pensant qui puisse concevoir un doute sur son innocence, puisque l'Histoire qui retiendra son nom et sa légendaire aventure a déjà rendu d'avance son jugement.

... L'autre 'Affaire' n'avait donc été gagnée ni perdue par personne. Nous n'avions pas réussi la rénovation révolutionnaire; les chefs de la Résistance[1] n'avaient pas détruit la République, ne l'avaient pas asservie à la tradition. La crise avait eu beau parcourir la surface de violents et longs remous, elle n'avait pas ébranlé le pays dans ses profondeurs. Une fois le cyclone passé, la France se retrouvait à peu près identique à elle-même. Etrange spectacle, qui prêterait à bien des réflexions amères,

[1] Resistance is Blum's word for the extreme anti-Dreyfusism which threatened the régime.

qui déçoit, qui pourrait presque décourager de l'action. Quoi! des années durant, une passion sans exemple avait possédé, bouleversé les vies personnelles et la vie commune! On s'était senti différent; tout avait semblé différent autour de soi. Et voilà que sitôt terminée la période aiguë, sitôt la température tombée, la société, le corps politique, les groupes, les individus se retrouvaient pareils à eux-mêmes, tels que s'il ne s'était rien passé!

LÉON BLUM: *Souvenirs sur l'Affaire*, Gallimard, 1935, pp. 174-7.

Dreyfusard Heroes

1. The Idealists: Péguy

Charles Péguy wrote Notre Jeunesse *in 1910 for the 'Cahiers de la Quinzaine', a series of books and essays which he himself had founded. It is a brilliant and poetic analysis of the Affair. He saw it as a major crisis for Judaism, Christianity and France, and in his taut repetitive style he praises those who rose with courage and self-sacrifice to the demands of the crisis and condemns those who turned it to their own political or social advantage. Bernard Lazare is his great hero for his selfless service to the Jewish cause. Emile Combes is one of the villains for his intolerant use of the Dreyfusard victory. But Péguy keeps most of his condemnation for Jaurès, who, he states, allowed the great cause of Dreyfusism to be submerged and extinguished in the politics of the Bloc des Gauches. The noble ideals of justice and truth were betrayed. From this accusation Péguy derives the generalisations put forward in this extract. 'Everything begins in mystique and ends in politics.' The important question, he says, is not whether one set of politics should triumph over another but that the mystique or ideals of a movement should not be killed by the politics which follow. True republicans should remain true republicans, and true royalists should remain true royalists. The true Dreyfusards, he continues, are those who retained their ideals, firstly, by fighting their enemies, and secondly, by refusing to submit (like Jaurès had done) to the politics into which the Dreyfusard cause degenerated. These were the heroes, and despite the power of the politicians, they have not betrayed their mystique.*

Vous nous parlez de la dégradation républicaine, c'est-à-dire, proprement, de la dégradation de la mystique républicaine en politique républicaine. N'y a-t-il pas eu, n'y a-t-il pas d'autres dégradations. Tout commence en mystique et finit en politique. Tout commence par *la* mystique, par une mystique, par sa (propre) mystique et tout finit par *de la* politique. La question, importante, n'est pas, il est important, il est intéressant que, mais l'intérêt, la question n'est pas que telle politique l'emporte sur telle ou telle autre et de savoir qui l'emportera de toutes les politiques. L'intérêt, la question, l'essentiel est que *dans chaque ordre, dans chaque système* LA MYSTIQUE NE SOIT POINT DÉVORÉE PAR LA POLITIQUE À LAQUELLE ELLE A DONNÉ NAISANCE.

L'essentiel n'est pas, l'intérêt n'est pas, la question n'est pas que telle ou telle politique triomphe, mais que dans chaque ordre, dans chaque système chaque mystique, cette mystique ne soit point dévorée par la politique issue d'elle.

En d'autres termes il importe peut-être, il importe évidemment que les républicains l'emportent sur les royalistes ou les royalistes sur les républicains, mais cette importance est infiniment peu, cet intérêt n'est rien en comparaison de ceci: que les républicains demeurent des républicains: que les républicains soient des républicains.

Et j'ajouterai, et ce ne sera pas seulement pour la symétrie, complémentairement j'ajoute: que les royalistes soient, demeurent des royalistes. Or c'est peut-être ce qu'ils ne font pas en ce moment-ci même, où très sincèrement ils croient le faire le plus, l'être le plus.

... Les abonnés de ces cahiers, même aujourd'hui, après douze ans de morts, et de renouvellements annuels, se composent aujourd'hui encore pour les deux tiers, sont encore pour les deux tiers des anciens dreyfusards, des nouveaux dreyfusards, des dreyfusards perpétuels, des dreyfusards impénitents, des dreyfusards *mystiques*, des hommes de cœur, des petites gens, généralement obscurs, généralement pauvres, quelques-uns très pauvres, pour ainsi dire misérables, qui ont sacrifié deux fois leur carrière, leur avenir, leur existence et leur pain: une première fois pour lutter contre leurs ennemis, une deuxième fois pour lutter contre leurs amis; et combien n'est-ce pas plus difficile; une première fois pour résister à la politique de leurs ennemis, une deuxième fois pour résister à la politique de leurs amis; une première fois pour ne pas succomber à leurs ennemis, une deuxième fois pour ne pas succomber à leurs amis.

... Une première fois pour ne pas succomber à la démagogie de leurs ennemis, une deuxième fois pour ne pas succomber à la démagogie de leurs amis; une première fois pour ne pas succomber à l'inimitié, une deuxième fois pour ne pas succomber à la plus difficile amitié.

Tous nous savons ce que ça nous a coûté. Et c'est pour cela que nous exigerons toujours de nos amis un respect que nos ennemis ne nous ont jamais refusé.

Les politiciens veulent que nous endossions leurs politiques, que nous marchions dans leurs politiques, dans leurs combinaisons, que nous entrions dans leurs vues, politiques, que nous trahissions nos mystiques pour leurs politiques, pour les politiques correspondantes, pour les politiques issues. Mais nous ne sommes pas sous leurs ordres.

C. PÉGUY: *Notre Jeunesse* (1st edn. 1910), Gallimard, 1933, pp. 27–8, 40–1.

2. The Socialists and the Proletariat:- Zévaès

The writings of Alexander Zévaès bear the mark of the socialism which was his own political creed. In particular, he pays homage to his mentor and hero Jean Jaurès. His colourful history of the Affair is a partisan one, repeating Reinach's accusations against the Jesuits and totally exaggerating the rôle of the working class. As a Jaurèsite version it has great interest. It is entirely contrary to Péguy's conclusions. The very politics which Péguy condemned are presented by Zévaès as the most progressive achievement of the Affair. In his conclusion reproduced here he admits that there were some sincere, if misguided, men among the anti-Dreyfusards, while among the opponents of injustice and arbitrary rule were the members of the proletariat, equally sincere but more impartial. The revisionist cause was led by socialists. Some young idealists became disillusioned: Péguy expected a great regeneration of mankind, and Halévy bemoaned the twilight of the Dreyfusard world. They were adolescents. In summary, the Dreyfusard movement was aimed at clericalism and militarism; 'Down with the army and the church' (goupillon— a holy-water sprinkler), and the Affair showed the spontaneous rising of the people for justice.

Et certes, dans ces deux camps, il y a incontestablement une masse d'honnêtes citoyens qui se donnent tout entiers à leur cause. Du côté nationaliste les chefs sont des faussaires, des complices des faussaires, des approbateurs et des glorificateurs des faux: il y a des Cavaignac et des Gonse, des Henry et des Esterhazy. Mais il y a aussi des hommes qui, de bonne foi par une conception étrange du patriotisme, s'imaginent défendre l'honneur de l'armée, qui considèrent que la campagne entreprise contre les décisions des Conseils de Guerre et contre l'Etat-Major est de nature à affaiblir l'organisme de la défense nationale et qui ne permettent pas qu'on y touche. Ils sont sincères. Mais ces milliers de prolétaires, d'humbles salariés de l'atelier et de l'usine qui, mus par un idéal de justice, ont embrassé la cause de l'officier israélite et millionnaire, qui eux-mêmes, si souvent dépouillés de la violation des prescriptions légales contre la juridiction et le huis clos des Conseils de Guerre, qui veulent que la justice soit entourée de toutes les garanties sans lesquelles ses arrêts seraient dépourvue d'autorité et de force, combien, eux aussi, ils sont sincères dans leurs passions et par-dessus tout, désintéressés...

C'est contre le danger représenté par le nationalisme et l'antisémitisme que dès la première heure, entre en ligne la prolétariat dans ses éléments les plus hardis et les plus clairvoyants....

Et après les socialistes conduits par Jaurès, Allemane, Gérault, Richard, c'est le gros des troupes républicains qui, s'ébranlant peu à peu, vont au combat — à un combat où la coalition monarchiste, nationaliste et antisémite menace directement la forme républicaine.

... Quelques jeunes gens, que le souci de la justice, la foi dans un idéal, plus ou moins imprécis, de vérité et d'émancipation, la parole vibrante de Jaurès, avaient entraînés dans la bataille, en sont sortis désillusionnés, déçus, découragés. Il faut lire en ce sens les pages de Charles Péguy, *Notre Jeunesse*, enregistrant ses rancœurs de croyant désabusé, ses déconvenues de militant dreyfusard.... Il avait entrevu dans l'Affaire l'aube d'une révolution sociale, et par là il entendait moins une transformation économique qu'une vaste rénovation humaine, morale, religieuse, mystique, élevant soudainement toutes les âmes dans les voies sereines de la bonté et de la beauté. Le brusque dénouement gouvernemental de l'Affaire—l'amnistie imposée par Waldeck-Rousseau—lui paraît un avortement lamentable, et c'est peut-être dans l'amertume alors éprouvée qu'il faut placer la raison de la conversion qui le ramène au catholicisme de son enfance et le conduit au seuil de l'Action Française.

Pareil désenchantement chez un autre revisionniste de la même génération, venu au dreyfusisme et au socialisme de Jaurès par la porte israélite: Daniel Halévy. Dans son *Apologie pour notre passé* écrite en 1910 il se demande 'D'où vient, qu'ayant été si heureux si fiers, d'où vient qu'il nous inspire aujourd'hui un mouvement si faible?'...

Mais ce sont là des illusions de grands enfants qui, dans l'enthousiasme de la vingtième année, demandaient à l'Affaire Dreyfus plus qu'elle ne pouvait donner...

Le mouvement Dreyfusard avait une double caractéristique.

D'abord, il était dirigé contre la Congrégation et l'Église romaine. Et sur ce point il a en partie réussi...

Et puis en même temps que contre la domination cléricale le mouvement dreyfusard était dirigé contre la puissance militaire, contre l'État-Major. A bas le sabre et le goupillon! telle était à l'époque l'expression courante.

... Mais plus que tout cela, le résultat de l'Affaire Dreyfus c'est d'avoir montré un peuple levé pour une idée de justice, mobilisé pour que la justice soit rendue à un seul. Quelle leçon! Et comment et pourquoi ce peuple ne se lèverait-il pas, demain, pour que la justice soit rendue à tous, à toutes les victimes de l'iniquité sociale?

A. ZÉVAÈS: *L'Affaire Dreyfus*, Editions de la Nouvelle Revue Critique, 1931, pp. 207–14.

The Affair as Light and Darkness

1. Triumph of Justice: Weil

The German historian Bruno Weil obtained from the family of the Count von Munster, the German Ambassador in Paris at the time of the Affair, a letter from Schwartzkoppen in which he mentioned his relations with Esterhazy. Armed with this important document, he published a history of the Affair in 1930 and thereby provoked the publication of Schwartzkoppen's Carnets *(see above, p. 120). Weil treated the Affair in its detective-story aspect and showed the events unfolding to bring justice and light. His preface and epilogue quoted here reveal his line of approach. He compares the Affair to the Calas case in the eighteenth century. A young man is found hanged; his father, a Protestant, is accused of opposing his son's interest in Catholicism and of murdering him. The father is found guilty and brutally executed. His widow interests Voltaire in her husband's innocence, and the great writer succeeds in securing his posthumous acquittal. The Affair is another case of 'guilty or innocent?' In retrospect, it was the struggle between the rights of the individual and the power of authority. Its outcome has brought hope to every innocent prisoner.*

Le 13 octobre 1761 on trouve à Toulouse un jeune homme pendu, dans le rez-de-chaussée de sa maison. Toulouse: une ville extrêmement catholique; le jeune homme, fils d'un père et d'une mère tous deux protestants, est connu pour incliner vers le catholicisme. Le père, âgé de soixante-deux ans, citoyen irréprochable, est arrêté; on lui fait un procès et, bien qu'à une faible majorité, le parlement de Toulouse rend la sentence: 'Jean Calas est coupable d'avoir tué son fils: il est condamné à mort. Il est condamné à être rompu vif et mourra sur la roue.'

Le jugement est exécuté. La veuve d'abord inculpée de complicité, puis remise en liberté, élit domicile à Genève où elle fait la connaissance de Voltaire. Voltaire, le railleur spirituel, le grand penseur, la plus grande puissance intellectuelle de son époque, entreprend la lutte pour la révision du jugement rendu à tort. Pendant trois années il inonde la France et la libre Suisse de ses pamphlets. En 1765, quatre ans après l'exécution, le Roi, ainsi que le conseil du Roi, reconnaissent à l'unanimité que Jean Calas a été condamné à mort quoique innocent. Sa veuve et ses héritiers sont remis en possession de ses biens. Mais la vie ne peut lui être restituée.

Cent trente ans plus tard, une nouvelle affaire fait frémir non seulement la France mais le monde entier: une affaire soulevant à nouveau l'éternelle question 'coupable ou innocent?' en tout son poids écrasant, avec ses problèmes d'une difficulté toujours renouvelée, avec toutes ses angoisses, ses poursuites acharnées et avec le souci du bonheur ainsi que du droit humain.

... L'Affaire ... était la querelle toujours renouvelée entre le Pouvoir et le Droit. La lutte entre la raison d'État et le sentiment humain. La question: où cessent les droits de l'individu, — où commencent ceux de la communauté?

... Et voilà le sens suprême du cas Dreyfus: il donne de l'espoir à tout innocent condamné à tort: il est la preuve classique de la possibilité d'une réparation du tort commis: il est le rayon consolateur tombant dans les prisons.

BRUNO WEIL: *L'Affaire Dreyfus* (translated from the German), Gallimard, 1930, Preface and Epilogue.

2. Progress of Democracy: Charensol

The history of the Affair by G. Charensol was the first account to appear in France after the publication of Schwartzkoppen's Carnets. *It was mostly impartial, but the conviction of the author that the Dreyfusard cause was a surge of truly democratic fervour is unconcealed. In this extract he draws the moral for his own time. The democratic basis of France, he states, is not exactly threatened, but the great ideals of our fathers seem commonplace to those who did not experience their vitality. A régime can be eroded as well as overthrown: its defenders must be vigilant.*

Sans supposer un seul instant que les concepts sociaux et politiques qui sont à la base de notre démocratie puissent un jour subir quelque atteinte, il faut reconnaître pourtant que, dans l'amollissement du succès, l'évolution sociale du régime s'est fortement ralentie au cours de ces dernières années. Les idées qui paraissaient à nos pères si authentiques prennent un aspect de poncif. Les jeunes générations qui n'ont point vu les luttes qu'il fallut soutenir pour les imposer, sentent mal peut-être leur vivante actualité.

Sans doute le régime n'a-t-il besoin d'être défendu de la même façon que naguère, mais un long travail d'érosion est quelque fois plus dangereux qu'un brutal coup de force. Souhaitons que la vigilance de ceux qui savent comprendre les leçons de l'histoire contemporaine ne s'endorme point.

G. CHARENSOL: *L'Affaire Dreyfus et la Troisième République*, Editions Kra, 1930, pp. 190–1.

3. The Sabotage of France: Maurras

The most consistent accusation of Charles Maurras against the Dreyfusards was that they had divided the nation, sapped its energies and undermined its power. In his memoirs, dedicated to the latest royalist pretender, he ignored the revelations of Schwartzkoppen and reiterated the interpretation of Dutrait-Crozon that Esterhazy was the mere accomplice of Dreyfus. But he is not really interested in who was the traitor nor, as he begins here, does he wish to enter the old debate of who was patriotic and who was in error. He states that he has little sympathy for those who were misguided or disillusioned. His thoughts lie rather with the dead of 1914–18, for whom the moral weakness provoked by the Affair was responsible. Every time he remembers the Affair he sees the children of France badly equipped in the war, dying helplessly at the front. Those who were coldly responsible for weakening France in this way have his eternal curses.

Ceux qui racontent cette histoire ont aujourd'hui coutume de mettre tout le monde d'accord en faisant admirer, comme une seule et même vertu, le feu jumeau des passions de justice et de patriotisme qui brillèrent alors d'un éclat symétrique au cœur des Français. Je ne dirai rien de pareil parce que je ne veux pas sacrifier aux faux dieux. La justice n'était pas d'un côté, ni la patrie de l'autre. Nous les défendions toutes deux. Je n'ai pas beaucoup de pitié pour ceux qui s'y sont laissé tromper. Non que je n'aie point vu de belles âmes ou de bons cœurs emportés contre tout bon sens dans les idées fausses et les romans. Tant pis pour ces victimes, car il y en a eu de plus intéressantes. ... Je songe au carnage de 1914-18 dans lequel la grave faiblesse morale de 1897-98-99 eut sa responsabilité. Là, j'ai un souvenir strictement contemporain.

Toutes les fois que cette fable de la victime d'une erreur judiciaire m'était réassenée avec des trémolos qui m'écœurent encore, je distinguais en esprit un champ de bataille sans doute moins spacieux et moins affreux que ne devait l'aménager la plus grande des guerres, mais enfin, et à la mesure de mon imagination j'y voyais la jonchée funèbre de ces beaux enfants de la France 'couchés froids et sanglants sur leur terre mal défendue' parce que, l'émeute orientale ayant renversé le rempart et brisé les armes, ils opposaient à l'artillerie leurs poitrines nues. Ce million et demi de morts et de mourants fait un rude charnier. Ceux qui l'ont élevé ou accru par sotte imprudence ne sont pas encore assez repentis pour émouvoir la miséricorde. Quant à ceux qui froidement, par politique ou fanatisme avaient monté cette mystification sanguinaire, leur bande ne finira pas d'encaisser nos malédictions.

CHARLES MAURRAS: *Au signe de Flore*, Collection 'Hier', 1931, pp. 59-60.

Suggested Reading

1. Background and Contextual

D. W. BROGAN: *The Development of Modern France*. London, Hamish Hamilton, 1940.
> A penetrating, lively study of the Third Republic—particularly good on 1870–1914. Examines the major crises as threats to the Republic.

F. GOGUEL: *La Politique des Partis sous la IIIe République*. Paris, Editions du Seuil, 1958.
> Brings clarity to the bewildering party changes and alignments. Good chapter on the political consequences of the Affair.

D. THOMSON: *Democracy in France*. London, O.U.P., 3rd edn., 1958.
> An excellent analysis of movements and political traditions in the Third Republic. A valuable start towards discovering the social bases of politics. Short but interesting on Vichy and the Fourth Republic.

G. WRIGHT: *France in Modern Times*. London, Murray, 1962.
> A study through to the Fifth Republic with considerable perception into the ideas and political mœurs of postwar France.

A. WERTH: *France 1940–1955*. London, Readers Union, 1957.
> Full of anecdotes which are always illuminating. He faces most of the difficult questions. Excellent critique of Maurras, Pétain and Laval.

R. ARON: *The Vichy Régime 1940–44*, trans. by H. Hare. London, Putnam, 1958.
> The standard critical history. The dilemmas as well as the illusions of the collaborators are thoughtfully examined.

H. MICHEL: *Histoire de la Résistance en France*. Paris, P.U.F., 1962.
> Perhaps too much organisational detail, but a useful short guide to the failures and successes of the Resisters: not so good on their ideals.

P. WILLIAMS and M. HARRISON: *De Gaulle's Republic*. London, Longmans, 1960.
> The title is indicative of the approach—the new phenomenon of a one-man republic and its relation to its predecessor is skilfully examined. Excellent on the Algerian problem.

2. The Affair

P. MIQUEL: *L'Affaire Dreyfus*. Paris, P.U.F., 1961.
   Easily the best history of the Affair: an amazing wealth of information in a short book and wide references to other interpretations.

G. CHAPMAN: *The Dreyfus Case: A Reassessment*. London, Hart-Davis, 1955.
   Describes the progress of the case with great accuracy, sustaining interest by its clarity and its insight into the main characters. Essentially an exciting drama, but a good general chapter on the Dreyfusian Revolution.

N. HALASZ: *Captain Dreyfus: Story of a Mass Hysteria*. New York, Simon and Schuster, 1955.
   A fast-moving re-creation of the Affair as it caught the public imagination. The analysis is of a lower quality than the narration.

P. BOUSSEL: *L'Affaire Dreyfus et la Presse*. Paris, Armand Colin, 1960.
   An anthology of extracts bearing on the case, rather than expressing social and political tensions, but the clash of opinion comes through. Remarkable set of cartoons which are more expressive.

M. BAUMONT: *Aux sources de l'Affaire*. Paris, Productions de Paris, 1959.
   Unusual aspects of the Affair from diplomatic documents. A judicious book which raises the interesting question—could the Germans have prevented the Affair?

S. THALHEIMER: *Die Affäre Dreyfus*. Munich, dtv, 1963.
   An exhaustive collection of documents on the successive stages of the case translated into German.

M. THOMAS: *L'Affaire sans Dreyfus*. Paris, Fayard, 1961.
   Despite its length, this is highly readable, with many light, incidental observations on men who have hitherto been shadowy figures like Schwartzkoppen himself. It asks the question—who really were the guilty among the officers? Excellent on Esterhazy.

3. Personalities

J. H. JACKSON: *Clemenceau and the Third Republic*. London, E.U.P., 1946.
   An entertaining little book. Traces Clemenceau's development to the height of power with objective understanding.

H. GOLDBERG: *Life of Jean Jaurès*. Madison, University of Wisconsin Press, 1962.
>The comparisons between Jaurès and other socialists are clearly made. There is a tendency to simplify.

A. ZÉVAÈS: *Le Cinquantenaire de J'accuse*. Paris, Fasquelle, 1948.
>Shows how Zola became a Dreyfusard and attempts to answer the more difficult question—Why?

D. W. BROGAN: *French Personalities and Problems*. London, Hamish Hamilton, 1946.
>His portraits of Barrès and Maurras and his analysis of their different nationalisms are quite excellent.

D. HALÉVY: *Péguy and the Cahiers de la Quinzaine,* trans. Ruth Bethell, London, Dobson, 1946.
>A sensitive literary portrayal with plenty of original Péguy. The Affair has only a short mention. Particularly acute on Péguy's Catholicism and nationalism and on his rebellious nature.

M. CURTIS: *Three against the Third Republic*. Princeton U.P., 1959.
>Ambitious project to link Maurras, Barrès and Sorel, but many of the comparisons are fruitful. Best on Sorel.

C. DELHORBE: *L'Affaire Dreyfus et les Ecrivains français*. Paris, Victor Attinger, 1932.
>In appearance a daunting book, but in content eminently rewarding, especially on Anatole France, Barrès and Péguy. The Affair here really is a catalyst.

G. D. PAINTER: *Marcel Proust*, Two Vols. London, Chatto and Windus, 1959.
>Great entertainment and impressive scholarship. The world of Proust has never been so colourfully drawn.

D. CAUTE: *Communism and French Intellectuals*. London, Deutsch, 1964.
>A number of impressive case studies of a phenomenon recurrent in French life. His generalisations on intellectual involvement are particularly valuable.

4. *Antisemitism*

R. F. BYRNES: *Antisemitism in Modern France. Prologue to Dreyfus*. New Brunswick, Rutgers, 1950.
>The best book on the Jewish problem in France. One looks forward to a second volume on the Affair, although many of the participants are discussed here.

E. SILBERNER: *French Socialism and the Jewish Question 1865-1914* Historia Judaica, April 1954.
> A much neglected aspect of antisemitism. He discusses socialists who were not antisemites as well as those who were.

H. ARENDT: *The Burden of our Time*. London, Secker, 1951.
> She is too inclined to exaggerate the rôle of Catholicism in the Affair, but her analysis of antisemitism is always stimulating and should be read for its wider European significance.

J. P. SARTRE: *Réflexions sur la Question Juive*. Paris, Gallimard, 1954.
> What many will find the most convincing philosophical and psychological explanation of antisemitism.

5. Catholicism

L. CAPÉRAN: *L'Anticléricalisme et l'Affaire Dreyfus*. Toulouse, Imprimerie Régionale, 1948.
> A little-used book which should be a first priority. Perhaps too much of an apology but a vital corrective to many anticlerical presuppositions. Good on the Leagues.

A. DANSETTE: *Religious History of Modern France*. Freiburg, Herder, 1961.
> The most objective and informative study of French Catholicism. The chapter on the Affair should be read in the context of those on the Ralliement and Christian Democracy.

Note also those that are marked for further reading in the Index to Sources.

INDEX TO SOURCES

Those with an asterisk are selected as particularly valuable for further reading.

Unless marked otherwise the place of publication is Paris.

AJALBERT, J. *La Forêt noire*, 1899.	86
BAILLY, PÈRE V. DE P. ('Le Moine'). *La Croix*, 8 February 1898.	63
BARRÈS, M. Letter to Maurras, in C. Maurras, *Enquête sur la Monarchie*.	110
*BARRÈS, M. *Scènes et doctrines du Nationalisme*, Vol. I, Plon, 1902.	36
*BLUM, L. *Souvenirs sur l'Affaire*, Gallimard, 1935.	122
BRUGERETTE, ABBÉ, *see* Saint Poli	
BRUNETIÈRE, F. *La Nation et l'Armée*, Bureaux de 'la Patrie Française', 26 April 1899.	46
BURNICHON, P. J. 'La Question du Jour', *Etudes*, 5 December 1898.	79
CHARENSOL, G. *L'Affaire Dreyfus et la 3ᵉ République*, Editions Kra, 1930.	128
*CLEMENCEAU, G. *L'Iniquité*, Stock, 1899, Préface.	34
CONYBEARE, F. C. *The Dreyfus Case*, London, George Allen, 1898.	85
Croix, la. 'Feu Ouvert', 8 February 1898.	63
DRUMONT, E. 'L'Ame de Dreyfus', *La Libre Parole*, 26 December 1894.	58
DUTRAIT-CROZON, H. *Précis de l'Affaire Dreyfus*, Nouvelle Librairie Nationale, 1909.	111
FAURE, S. *Les Anarchistes et l'Affaire Dreyfus*, Lafont, 1898.	106
FRANCE, A. *Discours prononcé aux funérailles d'Emile Zola*, 5 October 1902.	23
FRANCE, A. *L'Ile des Pingouins*, Clamann Lévy, 1925.	80
FRÉMONT ABBÉ. In Agnes Siegfried. *L'abbé Frémont*, Félix Alcan, 1932, vol. II, p. 166.	86
GOHIER, U. *L'armée contre la Nation*, Editions de la Revue Blanche, 1898.	43
*HALÉVY, D. *Apologie pour notre passé*, Cahiers de la Quinzaine, 1910.	113
HERZL, T. 'La situation en France', *Die Welt*, 24 December 1897.	65
JAURÈS, J. Speech in the Chamber, 22 January 1898.	97
*JAURÈS, J. *Les Preuves*, La Petite République, 1898.	103
LEMAZURIER, J. *Catéchisme Dreyfusard*, Stock, 1898	105
LEVY, LOUIS. *L'Univers Israélite*, 21 January 1898.	61
Manifeste des députés socialistes au prolétariat, 19 January, 1898.	99
*MARTIN DU GARD, R. *Jean Barois*, Nouvelle Revue Française, 1917.	20
MATHIEU MGR. In Agnes Siegfried, *L'abbé Frémont*, Félix Alcan, vol. II, 1932.	77
MAURRAS, C. 'Le Premier Sang. II', *La Gazette de France*, 7 September 1898.	41
MAURRAS, C. *Enquête sur la monarchie*, Versailles, Bibliothèque des œuvres politiques, 1928.	107
*MAURRAS, C. *Au signe de Flore*, Collection Hier, 1931.	129
*MEYER, A. *Ce que mes yeux ont vu*, Plon, 1911.	68

INDEX TO SOURCES

MORÈS, MARQUIS DE. In L'Archiviste, *Drumont et Dreyfus*, Stock, 1898. — 57
MUN, ALBERT DE. Speech in the Chamber, 4 December 1897. — 95
PÉGUY, C. 'Letter to Millerand', 13 January 1898. *Figaro Littéraire*, 4 June 1960. — 102
*PÉGUY, C. *Notre Jeunesse*, Gallimard, 1933. — 123
QUILLARD, P. *Le Monument Henry*, Stock, 1899. — 82
*REINACH, J. *Histoire de l'Affaire Dreyfus*, Fasquelle, 1903. — 83
ST AULAIRE, Comte de. *Confession d'un vieux diplomate*, Flammarion, 1953. — 77
SAINT-POLI, H. (abbé Brugerette). *L'Affaire Dreyfus et la Mentalité Catholique en France*, Storck, 1904. — 87
*SCHWARTZKOPPEN, COLONEL. *Carnets*. Editions Rieder, 1930. — 120
*SOREL, G. *La Révolution Dreyfusienne*, Marcel Rivière, 1909. — 24
Univers et Le Monde, L', 10 October 1899. — 78
Univers Israélite, L', 21 January 1898. — 61
VEUILLOT, E. *L'Univers et le Monde*, 10 October 1899. — 78
WEIL, B. *L'Affaire Dreyfus*, Gallimard, 1930, Préface, Epilogue. — 127
*WERTH, A. *France 1940–55*, London, Reader's Union, 1957. — 29
ZÉVAÈS, A. *L'Affaire Dreyfus*, Editions de la Nouvelle Revue Critique, 1931. — 125
ZOLA, E. *Lettre à la France*, 6 January 1898. — 81
ZOLA, E. 'J'accuse', *L'Aurore*, 13 January 1898. — 18
ZOLA, E. Speech at his Trial, 21 February 1898. — 38

INDEX

Action Française, 17, 29
Ajalbert, Jean, 10, 86
Aragon, Louis, 16
Astier, Emmanuel d', 16
Aurore, L', 8, 11, 13, 18–20, 31, 34, 44, 115
Autant, Edouard, 13
Autorité, L', 89

Bailly, Père Vincent de Paul, 11, 63–65, 73
Bainville, Jacques, 16
Barbusse, Henri, 16
Barrès, Maurice, 1, 11, 13, 15, 28, 29, 32, 36–8, 41, 59, 110
Becket, Thomas à, 120
Benjamin, Réné, 29
Bernis, Comte de, 99
Billot, General, 18, 82, 95
Bismarck, Otto von, 3
Blum, Léon, 16, 31, 36, 57, 117–18, 122–3
Boisdeffre, General, 7, 18, 19, 73, 95
Boulanger, General, 4, 15, 31, 34, 90, 94
Bourget, Paul, 32
Brisson, Henri, 13, 92
Broglie, Duc Albert de, 3, 32
Brugerette, Abbé, 2, 75, 76, 87–9
Brunetière, Ferdinand, 12, 14, 32, 46–49, 50, 105
Buffet, André, 107–9

Cahiers de la Quinzaine, 113, 123
Caillavet, Mme de, 15
Calas, Jean, 119, 120, 127–8

Camus, Albert, 16
Capéran, Louis, 73
Carrière, Eugène, 31
Cavaignac, General, 32, 91, 103, 125
Chaine, Léon, 75
Charensol, G., 117, 128–9
Charles I, 119
Charpentier, Armand, 117
Christiani, Baron, 93
Clemenceau, Georges, 5, 6, 7, 8, 11, 13, 20, 30, 34–6, 43, 76, 91, 93, 94, 110, 111, 115
Combes, Emile, 15, 28, 34, 76, 93, 95, 112, 123
Comité Catholique pour la Défense du Droit, 76, 87–9
Conybeare, Frederick, 85–6
Coppée, François, 32
Croix, La, 11, 28, 61, 63–5, 71, 73, 79, 111

Darnand, Joseph, 29
Daudet, Léon, 32
Daumier, Honoré, 12
Dausset, Louis, 32
Déat, Marcel, 29
Dégas, Edgar, 52
Delhorbe, Cécile, 115
Dépêche de Toulouse, La, 11, 76
Déroulède, Paul, 4, 5, 15, 93, 107
Doriot, Jacques, 29
Dreyfus, Captain Alfred, *passim*
Dreyfus, Mathieu, 8
Drumont, Edouard, 2, 5, 6, 10, 11, 15, 30, 50–6, 57, 58–60, 61, 70, 73, 86, 91, 111, 119

INDEX

Duclaux, Emile, 14, 31, 106
Dupuy, Charles, 90
Durkheim, Emile, 32
Dutrait-Crozon, Henri, 111–12, 129

Eclair, L', 11
Eluard, Paul, 16
Esterhazy, Count, 8, 9, 12, 18, 31, 92, 111, 117, 120–2, 125, 127, 129
Etudes, 79–80

Faure, Félix, 8, 15, 18, 93, 107
Faure, Sébastien, 106–7
Ferry, Jules, 3, 69
Figaro, Le, 44, 67, 89
Floquet, Charles, 5
Forain, J. L., 14
Forzinetti, Major, 13
France, Anatole, 15, 23–4, 31, 80–1, 114
Frémont, Abbé, 76, 86–7
Freystätter, Captain, 13
Fritel, Pierre, 13

Gambetta, Léon, 30, 94
Garnier, Abbé, 52
Gaulle, Charles de, 94
Gaulois, Le, 11
Gayraud, Abbé, 52
Gazette de France, La, 11, 12, 41–3
Gohier, Urbain, 28, 43–6, 52, 81
Grand-Carteret, J., 12
Grimaux, Edouard, 31
Guèsde, Jules, 56, 95, 99
Guyot, Yves, 11, 76, 85, 106

Halévy, Daniel, 31, 113, 118, 125, 126
Havet, Louis, 31
Henry, Colonel, 8, 9, 12, 41–3, 75, 92, 107, 118, 125
Hérédia, José Maria de, 32
Herr, Lucien, 15, 28, 36, 102, 103

Herz, Cornelius, 5
Herzl, Theodore, 65–8, 69

Intransigeant, L', 11

Jaurès, Jean, 6, 9, 11, 18, 23, 28, 30, 43, 56, 76, 91, 93, 97–9, 100, 102, 103–5, 106, 110, 117, 123, 125, 126
Journal, Le, 11
Judet, Ernest, 11, 86

Kahn, Zaddoc, 51, 60
Kaiser Wilhelm II, 117

Lac, Père du, 72–3, 84–5
Lacordaire, Père, 72, 75
Lafargue, Paul, 56
Langevin, Pierre, 31
Lazare, Bernard, 7, 8, 11, 13, 51, 91, 93, 106, 114, 119, 123
Leblois, Louis, 8, 117
Lemaître, Jules, 14, 28
Leo XIII, 5, 55, 71, 72, 73
Libre Parole, La, 6, 11, 54, 58–60, 62, 73, 75, 82, 103
Ligue Antisémite, 15, 54, 57
Ligue de la Patrie Française, 9, 12, 13, 14, 15–16, 31–2
Ligue des Droits de l'Homme, 9, 15–16, 31–2, 76, 106, 119
Ligue des Patriotes, 15, 93
Loubet, President, 93
Louys, Pierre, 32
Loynes, Comtesse de, 15, 28

MacMahon, General, 3
Malon, Benoît, 54
Malraux, André, 16
Martin du Gard, Roger, 11, 20–3
Mathieu, Mgr, 77–8, 86
Mauriac, François, 57, 118
Maurras, Charles, 11, 12, 16, 27, 28, 29, 30, 32, 41–3, 86, 92, 107–110, 112, 118, 119, 120, 129–30

138

INDEX

Mazel, Henri, 117
Méline, Jules, 71, 91, 92, 95, 119
Mercier, General, 7, 11, 18
Meyer, Arthur, 11, 15, 68–70
Michel, Louise, 106
Millerand, Alexandre, 93, 100, 102
Monet, Claude, 31
Monod, Gabriel, 7, 62
Montalembert, Comte de, 72, 75
Morès, Marquis de, 15, 57–8
Mun, Comte Albert de, 30, 68, 95–7, 102
Munster, Count von, 127

Napoleon I, 4, 10, 30, 43, 46
Nijinski, 115

Paléologue, Maurice, 118
Pasteur, Louis, 14
Paty de Clam, Lieutenant Colonel du, 18, 19
Péguy, Charles, 15, 24, 31, 32–4, 50, 51, 102, 113–14, 115, 118, 123–5, 126
Pellieux, General de, 18, 113
Pétain, Marshal, 10, 29
Petit Journal, Le, 11
Petite République, La, 11, 103
Pichot, Abbé, 76
Picquart, Colonel, 7, 8, 9, 50, 73, 111, 114
Piou, Jacques, 71, 75
Pius IX, 72
Pressensé, Francis de, 32
Prévost, Marcel, 15
Proust, Marcel, 1, 14, 31, 114, 115
Psichari, Jean, 31
Psst!, Le, 12

Quillard, Pierre, 75, 82–3

Radical, Le, 76
Ranc, Arthur, 7, 34, 42, 76

Ravary, Commandant, 18, 19
Reinach, Baron Jacques de, 5, 7
Reinach, Joseph, 7, 14, 28, 43, 60, 72, 79, 83–4, 102, 111, 112, 120, 125
Revue Blanche, 14
Revue des Deux Mondes, 14
Revue Socialiste, 54
Rochefort, Henri, 11
Roget, General, 93
Rolland, Romain, 16
Roque, Colonel de la, 29
Rousseau, Jean-Jacques, 28, 30

Sabatier, Guillaume, 11
Sartre, Jean-Paul, 16
Scheurer-Kestner, Auguste 7, 8, 10, 12, 14, 50, 62, 91, 93
Schwartzkoppen, Colonel, 6, 117, 120–2, 127
Séailles, Professor, 31
Seignobos, Professor Charles, 31
Siècle, Le, 11, 76, 85
Sifflet, Le, 12
Silberner, E., 52
Simon, Jules, 72
Soleil, Le, 89
Sorel, Georges, 24–5, 73, 90, 112–33, 114
Stock, P. V., 13, 73
Strauss, Mme, 14, 15
Stravinsky, Igor, 115
Syveton, Gabriel, 32

Taxil, Léo, 55
Thomas, Marcel, 118

Univers et Le Monde, L', 10, 78–9
Univers Israélite, L', 51, 56, 61–3, 76

Vaillant, Edouard, 99
Vallotton, F., 12
Vaugeois, Henri, 32
Vaughan, Ernest, 11

INDEX

Verne, Jules, 32
Viollet, Paul, 32, 76
Vogüé, Vicomte de, 32
Voltaire, François-Marie Arouet, 119, 127–8

Waldeck-Rousseau, René, 11, 73, 93, 95, 112, 126
Weil, Bruno, 119, 120, 127–8

Welt, Die, 65
Werth, Alexander, 29

Zévaès, Alexander, 114, 117, 118, 125–7
Zola, Emile, 8, 9, 11, 15, 18–25, 28, 30, 31, 38–41, 46, 63, 64, 71, 76, 81–2, 91, 93, 97, 106, 113, 114, 115, 118, 119

/DC 354 K37 00001

**Library and Learning
Resources Center
Bergen Community College**
400 Paramus Road
Paramus, N.J. 07652-1595

Return Postage Guaranteed